FOR SALE

BY JOHN FOSTER

HOW
BOOKS

Cincinnati, Ohio
www.howdesign.com

OVER 200 INNOVATIVE SOLUTIONS IN PACKAGING DESIGN

For more fine books from F+W Publications, visit www.fwpublications.com.

12 11 10 09 08   5 4 3 2 1

Distributed in Canada by Fraser Direct, 100 Armstrong Avenue, Georgetown,
Ontario, Canada L7G 5S4, Tel: (905) 877-4411. Distributed in the U.K. and
Europe by David & Charles, Brunel House, Newton Abbot, Devon, TQ12 4PU,
England, Tel: (+44) 1626 323200, Fax: (+44) 1626 323319, E-mail: postmaster@
davidandcharles.co.uk. Distributed in Australia by Capricorn Link, P.O. Box
704, Windsor, NSW 2756 Australia, Tel: (02) 4577-3555.

Library of Congress Cataloging-in-Publication Data

Foster, John, 1971-
   For sale : over 200 innovative solutions in packaging design / John Foster.
      p. cm.
   Includes bibliographical references and index.
   ISBN 978-1-60061-063-9 (hardcover : alk. paper)
   1. Packaging--Design. 2. Commercial art. I. Title.
   TS195.4.F67 2008
   658.5'64--dc22
                                                    2008019479

Edited by Amy Schell
Designed by John Foster
Art directed by Grace Ring
Production coordinated by Greg Nock

F+W PUBLICATIONS, INC.

About the Author

Special thanks to my family (as always) and everyone close to me who remains so supportive. The entire crew at fuszion (especially Rick!) and everyone I have ever worked beside—I learned something valuable from each and every one of you. Special thanks to everyone at HOW; Megan, Grace and especially Amy Schell who was willing to do this with me once again. Huge Foster kisses to all of you.

John Foster is Vice President, Creative, at Alexandria, Virginia-based fuszion. He is a frequent speaker on design and education issues and has appeared around the world, including sessions at the 2005, 2006 and 2008 HOW Design Conferences, the largest design gatherings in the world. He has also finished a recent tenure on the Fox River Paper Co. Designer Advisory Board and the Board of Directors of the Art Directors Club of Metropolitan Washington. John's work has received international recognition and has been featured in numerous books and magazines, including *Communication Arts*, *Print*, *Novum*, *HOW* and *Step 100* among others. His work has been included in galleries worldwide and was recently featured in the Smithsonian Museum of Design's Graphic Noise exhibit. He is also the recipient of a gold and silver medal from the Art Directors Club of Metropolitan Washington, as well as a Best of Show from the ADDYs.

In addition, John finds time to write and is the author of *New Masters of Poster Design* for Rockport Publishers, as well as *Maximum Page Design* for HOW Books. He has a new book for Sub Pop Records releasing in 2009.

He resides in a home he is constantly working on with his charming and beautiful wife and daughter and the world's goofiest foxhounds.

About fuszion

Fuszion is a national graphic design firm that specializes in marketing for the entertainment, advocacy and professional services industries. Their diverse range of clients provides a new learning experience at each and every turn that only serves to sharpen their skills for the next project. They have worked with global brands such as Warner Bros., Discovery, Coca-Cola, Fox, National Geographic, Chronicle Books and ESPN as well as important organiztions like the Smithsonian Institution, Americans for the Arts, Reading is Fundamental and many more.

Introduction

I am a consumer. Everything around me appears ready for my consumption. To be perfectly honest, I often just sit back in anticipation, waiting for air to be presented to me so I can inhale. How do I know everything is ready for my consumption, you may ask? Because the fancy box wrapped around the item I need or want tells me so. It says … just read me, just look at me, just touch me. It is sitting there upon the shelf begging for my attention. So perfectly formed to my desires (or is it the other way around, and do we really care if it is?) that I am certain it is only for me. Except there are rows and rows of items just like it, and they beckon those around me to join in as we partake in the pleasures that await us inside. How could a little label say so much? How could a cardboard box know me so well? How could a tube of aluminum cause my mouth to water underneath the phosphate sheen of this terrible lighting?

It's the packaging, silly!

It would be easy to diminish the power these tiny boxes, labels and cans hold on us. *Why, it's just the brand I grew up with. I happen to like the taste better. My favorite color is orange.* The excuses go on and on, but in the end, they must give in begrudgingly to the magic of packaging.

We have all sampled music by an artist we had never heard of based solely on some connection with the packaging. We have all tasted a drink based solely on the promise of a burst of refreshing flavor showcased on a shiny can. It is time to admit that packaging plays a big part in shaping our lives. Now more than ever, the world is being wrapped up in new and inventive ways, begging consumers to lay down their hard-earned money. In turn, we consumers have challenged manufacturers to continue to wow us as we pretend to be more visually savvy than the generation before us. If a quick glance through this book is any indication, they seem to be up to the task.

I have to admit that I am a design junkie, and often I spend far too much time trying to figure out who provided the design for the products I buy and admire. Because you have made it this far into the introduction, I would venture a guess that you share the same affliction. Well, wonder no more. What follows is a behind-the-scenes look at some of the most innovative packaging designers in the world. They will show you some of the interesting paths a product takes, from initial client meeting until placement on the shelf.

Ever wonder what it would be like to work for Mick Jagger? Stefan Sagmeister pulls back the curtain on page 2. Cleaning products seem like a design wasteland? Not in the hands of Sharon Werner on page 76. Just when you thought CD design couldn't get any cooler, check out Sub Pop Records on page 42, or young guns Invisible Creature on 112, design legend Art Chantry on page 86, or all the way from Israel, the striking work of Jewboy on page 95.

Thirsty? Soda gets a serious makeover courtesy of B.I.G. Ogilvy, New York, on page 51, and if you have a taste for the hard stuff, non●object will pour you a stiff one on page 99. If that drink has loosened up your sense of humor, Modern Dog has just the item to purchase on page 168. Then you might like a little chewing gum to help your breath, courtesy of Methane Studios on page 172. Or maybe you just found yourself in the mood for a set of Tom Jones DVDs from the gang at fuszion on page 63.

The work contained within this book shows just a small (yet brilliant) portion of what is out there. Packaging design has always been its own art form within the profession. Some simply cannot master the dimensional aspect or the selling power. At its essence, packaging is twice as hard as a normal design problem: You need to place yourself not only in the shoes of the client, but in those of the people reaching for the product, just dying to bring it home with them. Not an easy task by any means, despite the masterful executions you are about to view.

Consume. Enjoy.

JOHN FOSTER

Sagmeister, Inc. New York City

Number of employees: 1
Location: New York City
First year of business: 1993

Life with Stefan Sagmeister is rarely dull. Take the following story, for instance. "Sitting in the Taj Mahal Hotel in Bombay, a fax comes through from the office stating that the Rolling Stones' management called to have our work sent to their attention," he says. "I fax him a letter to be included when he sends the portfolio, emphasizing that we deliver on time and within budget. I hardly mentioned the work itself; it's there for them to see. Two weeks later, we get another call from their management, stating that the band liked the work and wants to meet. Soon, a brand-new stretch limo picks me up at the studio, the driver hands over business-class tickets for L.A., and I have a stupid grin on my face all the way to the airport. As I look out over the sun-drenched New Jersey industrial landscape with the Statue of Liberty at my back, I'm contemplating if this is one of those 'happy' moments that I have about once a year.

"They upgrade me to first class, I watch the first funny airline movie in ages and arrive at the Four Seasons in Beverly Hills. I go upstairs and smoke on the balcony. The next morning, I get a good sunburn at the pool, watching cartoony L.A. types wheeling and dealing in their bathing suits, shouting lines into their phones like, 'You've got to lay it on the line for them.' At 2:30, Jagger's assistant, Lucy, meets me in the bar, gives me a quick rundown on Mick and we go to the suite. In the elevator, I'm nervous.

"Mick opens the door, turns around immediately without saying hello, and I feel awkward. Lucy introduces us: He's friendly, but busy going through a Sotheby's catalog with Charlie Watts. They are checking out a Monet painting. 'At nine million, that's a real bargain,' Mick says in a heavy British accent. 'Pity I have no white walls left to hang it.'

"Mick grabs my portfolio and says, 'So, you're the floaty one.' 'The floaty one?' 'Yeah, all your covers seem to float in the plastic box.' He likes the Lou Reed package, likes the attention to detail in some of the others, and I can stop being nervous. He doesn't have a title for the album yet but promises to send over the music of three or four songs, including lyrics, next week. I ask him about his favorite Stones covers, and he mentions without hesitation: *Exile on Main St.*, *Sticky Fingers* and *Some Girls*.

"These are my favorites as well: 'We should have an easy time working together since I would have told you exactly the same covers, only in a different order: *Sticky Fingers*, *Some Girls* and *Exile on Main St.*' Charlie Watts (in a lowered voice) asks Jagger: 'What's ON *Sticky Fingers*?' to which Mick replies: 'Oh, you know Charlie, the one with the zipper, the one that Andy did.'

"The stupid happy grin is back on my face. I tell them I feel like I've won first prize in 'The-Big-Rolling-Stones-Meet-the-Band-All-Expenses-Paid' radio show contest. They laugh, and I am out of there. I meet with the stage designers and fly out at 8:30. I feel good and am asleep before the plane leaves the ground."

Designing for music was a major reason for the firm's existence, Sagmeister admits. "Like many designers my age, I became a designer because I wanted to design album covers." Unfortunately, it is a diminishing part of his portfolio. It used to be the main part of the business, but now it's only about 20 percent.

Very involved in every detail of his work, Sagmeister takes a hands-on approach. "I need to have a thorough understanding of [manufacturing] processes in order to design in them. Considering I had no education in industrial design, this often involves a lot of trial and error, many dummies and a lot of help from my friends." Once complete, these projects share a wonderful synchronicity with his travels. "The print numbers are often very high, so many of our packaging designs can be found in many different countries internationally." However, the creative in him does not disappear once the exterior is completed. In fact, "I would rather be responsible for the content than packaging said content," he admits.

Q. What would be your dream packaging job? It can be an existing product or something not yet created for retail …
A. A CD cover for King Crimson or the Coca-Cola can. (For very different reasons.)

Q. Do you still get excited when you see your design sitting on the shelf at a store?
A. If it's good, yes. If not, no.

Studio: Sagmeister, Inc.

Art Director: Stefan Sagmeister

Designers: Matthias Ernstberger, Roy Rub

Project Editor: Alex Steffen

Editor at Publisher: Deborah Aaronson

Client: Harry N. Abrams Inc.

Client's Services: book publisher

Size: 6⅝" x 9½"

Inks: (slipcase) five-color offset printing, laser die-cut

Cover: book boards wrapped in newsprint paper

Options Shown: one

Sagmeister explains that *Worldchanging* is a collection of reports about "new, positive developments in science, engineering, architecture, business and politics that will change this world. We designed this book to appeal not just to a core green audience, but to a wide spectrum of the general public. At the same time, it also holds special surprises for regular visitors to Worldchanging.com." In addition, the die-cut holes of the slipcase allow the sun to yellow the recycled paper of the cover over time, imprinting (and changing) the book cover itself.

Studio: Sagmeister Inc.

Art Director: Stefan Sagmeister

Designers: Hjalti Karlsson, Stephan Haas

Copy and Concept: Karen Salmansohn

Client: Blue Q

Inks: (perfume) one-color offset on art paper mounted on board, gloss laminated and die cut, acetate sleeve. (soap) one-color offset on coated matt art board, die cut.

Options Shown: one

"The concept, developed by writer Karen Salmansohn, was that Blue Q would sell a perfume with a separate little book, which talks about the philosophy of Unavailable. The idea is that you might be more desirable when you're unavailable—don't fake orgasm but do fake call waiting," explains Sagmeister. "Since so many perfumes are sold in gift packs where the customer gets a little bullshit item like a vanity case or a shower scrubber or a whatnot extra, I was very wary of the attached book, thinking it would only become another throwaway item." Instead, he drew on a project ten years in his past that inspired the book to become the packaging. He says, "The philosophy wraps the scent tightly."

"The black bar over the type was a rather obvious choice, influenced by censorship bars, information that is not available," he admits. "We printed the word itself only on the back of the bottle so the viewer has to tilt it for it to become available."

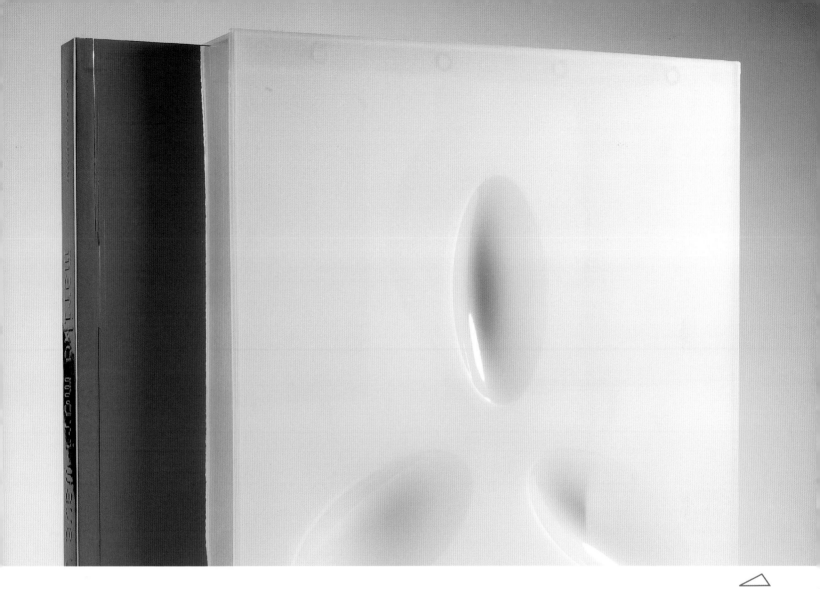

Mariko Mori's *Wave UFO* book is much more than a semitransparent slipcase. "The entire book focuses on only a single piece of art, but a rather complex one. Three people can enter the Wave UFO, have electrode headsets attached to their forehead and experience a 3-D animation changing in sync with their individual brain waves," explains Sagmeister.

Studio: Sagmeister Inc.

Art Director: Stefan Sagmeister
Designer: Matthias Ernstberger
Photographers: Richard Learoyd, Markus Tretter, Tom Powel, Red Saunders, Rudolf Sagmeister
Illustrator: Marcus Della Torre
Client: Kunsthaus Bregenz
Client's Services: public art fund
Printing Process: (slipcase) injection molding, (cover) luminescent foil over five-color offset
Options Shown: four

Studio: Sagmeister Inc.

Art Director: Stefan Sagmeister

Designer: Matthias Ernstberger

Illustrator: Matthias Ernstberger

Photographer: Kenvin Knight

Client: Universal Music Austria

Date: 2004

Printing Process: four-color offset, gloss matte lamination, four-color stickers

Options Shown: one

"The new album cover by the Austrian analog/digital musician Hans Platzgumer succeeds in producing a hovering underwater atmosphere. Fitting to this quiet but very aware soundscape, we designed an abstracted underwater world," says Sagmeister. Using the standard packaging for a vinyl record, the firm reinvented it by visual sleight of hand.

Studio: Sagmeister Inc.

Art Director: Stefan Sagmeister

Designer: Matthias Ernstberger

Cover Paintings: Vladimir Dubossarsky, Alexander Vinogradov

Creative Supervisor: Hugh Brown

Client: Rhino

Size: 16¾" x 5½"

Printing Process: four-color offset, cover matte laminated, elastic closure, 100-page booklet

Options Shown: "We first showed one, and it was killed. Then we showed one more."

"Titled *Once in a Lifetime* and containing three CDs and one DVD, this panoramic Talking Heads collection features cover paintings by the Russian contemporary artists Vladimir Dubossarsky and Alexander Vinogradov. [The paintings] contain all of my favorite visual icons: babies, bears, severed limbs and bare naked people, Except a guy in boxers on the inside front cover," marvels Sagmeister. "It contains over one hundred rare photographs and extensive essays. The extreme format of the packaging not only allows for easy storage in standard record store bins, but will also handily obstruct access to all CDs behind it."

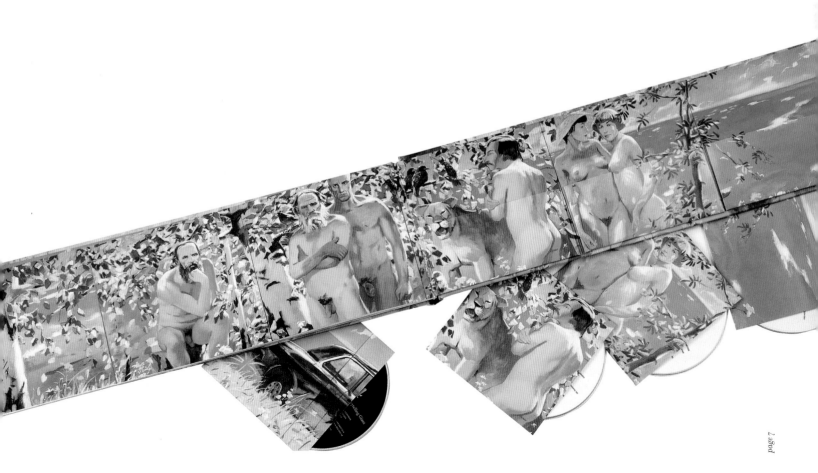

Studio: Sagmeister Inc.

Art Director: Stefan Sagmeister

Designer: Matthias Ernstberger

Illustrator: Matthias Ernstberger

Client: Capitol Records

Printing Process: four-color offset in jewel case

Options Shown: one

"OK Go is a young band from Chicago playing sophisticated pop music. If their music [were] a car, it would be a 1980s square Volvo—we asked," laughs Sagmeister.

Studio: Design Army

Art Directors: Pum Lefebure, Jake Lefebure

Designer: Lee Monroe

Client: Sophie Lefebure

Client's Services: being cute

Inks: four-color process

Printing Process: offset

Options Shown: one

Special Production Techniques: die cut, hand assembled and packaged

"Sophie Lefebure was turning one and, having designers as parents, she had to have a super-cool birthday party invite," admit the Lefebures. "The invitation is a set of hand-assembled blocks that have 'S, O, P, H, I, E' and the number '1' printed on the sides. So literally, Sophie is turning one! The blocks were then packaged in a custom vellum sheet that folds up to act as a carrier for the blocks. It took a lot of time to put the invites together, but Sophie only turns one once!"

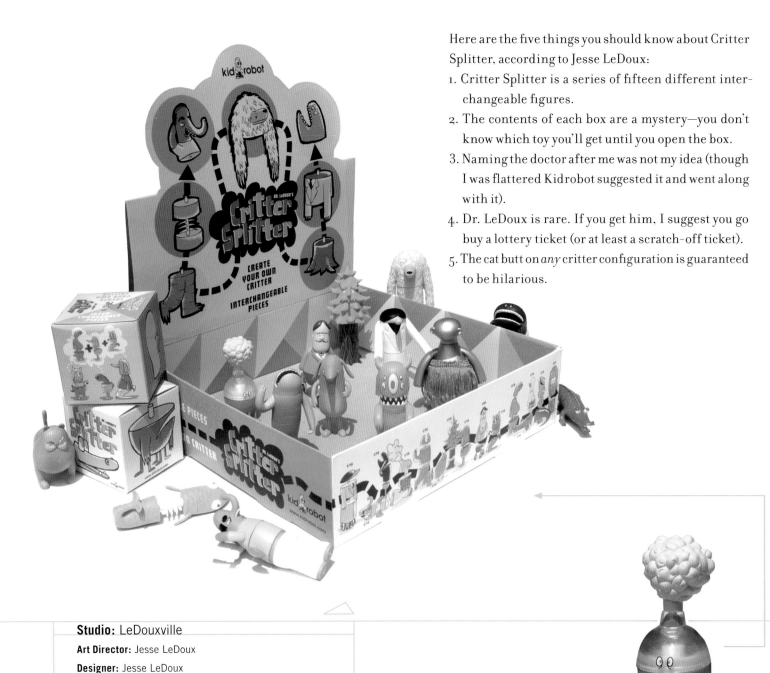

Here are the five things you should know about Critter Splitter, according to Jesse LeDoux:

1. Critter Splitter is a series of fifteen different inter-changeable figures.
2. The contents of each box are a mystery—you don't know which toy you'll get until you open the box.
3. Naming the doctor after me was not my idea (though I was flattered Kidrobot suggested it and went along with it).
4. Dr. LeDoux is rare. If you get him, I suggest you go buy a lottery ticket (or at least a scratch-off ticket).
5. The cat butt on *any* critter configuration is guaranteed to be hilarious.

Studio: LeDouxville

Art Director: Jesse LeDoux

Designer: Jesse LeDoux

Client: Kidrobot

Client's Services: designer toys

Illustrator: Jesse LeDoux

Inks: four-color process

Printing Process: offset

Options Shown: one

Studio: LeDouxville

Art Director: Kristine Ripley

Designer: Jesse LeDoux

Client: Drive-Thru Records

Client's Services: record label

Illustrator: Jesse LeDoux

Inks: four-color process

Printing Process: offset

Options Shown: one

"The band [Hellogoodbye] really wanted to do a coloring book-like CD package, so the listener could customize their CD package while listening to the music," says LeDoux. "My initial idea was to do fuzzy flocked printing (like the unicorn posters at the drug store when you were a kid), but it would have been too thick to insert into the CD jewel case. Round two involved inserting a crayon in the thin spine on the left side of the jewel case, but the pressing plant kept raising the insertion fee until it was no longer feasible. They adjusted the quote something like four times until they were able to find our breaking point!" he laments. "Just wait until the director's cut comes out ten years from now … it'll be flocked *and* have a crayon!"

Number of employees: 2
Location: Minneapolis, MN
First year of business: 2000

Wink Minneapolis

Looking through the portfolio of Minneapolis design firm Wink, I am continually amazed that two people in a room can produce such a perfect mix of simple typography applied in a classic manner, sophisticated imagery juxtaposed with fun and playful graphic imagery, and fresh new color combinations. Wink principals Scott Thares and Richard Boynton are geniuses at taking the familiar and making it inspirational and refreshing. These two take design and fun equally seriously. (Thares may very well qualify as a student of comedy.) Each partner embraces the joy of working on his own terms with someone he trusts and respects and allows it to color all they touch. Minneapolis is well known for its design, and in particular, its packaging. Standing out in such a tough crowd isn't always easy, but for Wink it is certainly well deserved.

"The ability to make something beautiful in the marketplace is very alluring," according to Thares and Boynton. Making things beautiful is something the boys at Wink know all about. "We believe that packaging is just a natural progression and extension of most design projects that we are involved with." Taking the lead from their masterful work in other areas, clients have sought them out to tackle their packaging problems.

Packaging design can come with its own set of hurdles though. "The long production lead times can be challenging on certain retail packages that are manufactured overseas," they admit. Not to mention the work they put into all of the "unknowns" that might crop up in fleshing out a client's identity and branding system. "Sometimes we create vendor style guides based on our package designs. Often, we are amazed when something is explicitly detailed, and then the execution is screwed up and the production is all wrong. When the finished piece hit stores shelves, it leaves us dumbfounded," they lament.

Their level of involvement on the actual production changes depending on the project. "It's all based on the client and budget," they explain. "We've done everything from specify the paper stock to oversee the printing process. We have even created die lines for the actual products." However for the projects that are large retail production runs that are printed overseas, "we generally create a vendor style guide that calls out the grid, colors, fonts and overall design direction so other production key lines that may not be executed (on our end) would be consistent (with the initial design)." They then have to sit back and hope that the guides will be followed, which can be nerve-racking.

Even with all of the inherent challenges, packaging keeps Wink pretty busy. "It all depends on the year: Some years it's about 50 percent of our business; other years it's around 25 percent," but they are always working on something for the retail shelves. Of course, this work is fit in between mustache-growing contests and making hilarious films starring KISS dolls (apologies—action figures) that explain the beginnings of their firm.

One thing is certain in the end: a unique solution. "Every job is different, therefore, every challenge is different," they say. In the end, however, the Wink dynamic duo attack every challenge with the same mix of smarts and fun that is so evident in their work—whether it is for the MTV Movie Awards or a pharmaceutical container of fish oil.

Q. What would be your dream packaging job? It can be an existing product or something not yet created for retail …
A. It would be something that would be in a can and could be purchased and consumed worldwide. And once ingested, it would cure cancer and bring about world peace … how's that for a dream?

Q. Do you still get excited when you see your design sitting on the shelf at a store?
A. Absolutely!

Studio: Wink

Art Directors: Richard Boynton, Scott Thares

Designer: Richard Boynton

Client: Daub & Bauble

Client's Services: personal and home care products

Illustrator: Richard Boynton

Inks: four PMS per fragrance

Printing Process: flexography

Options Shown: two

"Daub & Bauble was poised to be just another new entry in an already saturated market," explains Boynton. "The challenge was to create a point-of-difference among the product line that would help it stand out from the hundreds of other hand soaps, lotions and dish detergents." After research did little to distinguish it in the production and manufacturing stages, Wink started to feel the pressure. "The success of the brand all hinged on devising a unique strategy with a strong and resonant [visual] personality," he admits. "The solution came in the form of 'edition packaging.' Each of the three products has three fragrances, and each fragrance has three label patterns in modern, classic and even toile style. A set number of labels are printed per run, and once the supply has been depleted, a series of three new label patterns per fragrance will be introduced. And so on. This creates an almost 'objet d'art' quality surrounding each product." The final product builds excitement and anticipation. Not to mention, customers can even go online to vote for the next series of artwork.

Studio: Wink

Art Directors: Scott Thares, Richard Boynton

Designer: Scott Thares

Client: Target

Client's Services: retail store

Illustrator: Scott Thares

Inks: four-color process

Printing Process: offset

Options Shown: three

Creating the summer in-store campaign for Target, "Random Acts of Summer," Thares used photographic images from nature, such as water, grass and wood. According to Thares, "The packaging also used illustration-patterned images that were used on the seasonal products themselves, which are seen in the cloud, raindrop, fish and butterfly shapes. The look and feel of the layout grid for the entire packaging system was deliberately meant to be off-kilter and random. The project included over eighty SKUs of products. The summer seasonal packaging followed the overall campaign elements we created in-store."

Studio: Wink

Art Directors: Richard Boynton, Scott Thares

Designer: Richard Boynton

Client: J&B Wholesale

Client's Services: deli food

Illustrator: Richard Boynton

Inks: two PMS labels, one PMS paper tape

Printing Process: offset

Options Shown: one

For this project, Wink needed to create a packaging line for traditional deli products ranging from sliced meats to potato salad. According to Boynton, "The identity and packaging system for The Farmer in the Deli conveys a sense of homemade quality through its vernacular that falls somewhere between old recipe cards and vintage metal signs." To keep costs down, the system was basically made up of two-color labels that were adhered to stock plastic cartons, Ziploc bags and vacuum-sealed bags.

Studio: Wink

Art Directors: Richard Boynton, Scott Thares

Designer: Richard Boynton

Client: Marshall Field's

Client's Services: retail

Illustrator: Richard Boynton

Inks: multiple PMS for some, process color for others

Printing Process: offset

Options Shown: one

Special Production Techniques: printed metallic art on metallic foil for candy bars

Field's Sweet Spot was a nostalgic candy destination of the Midwest department store chain Marshall Field's [which has been purchased by Macy's since this project]. The look (a nod to the mod 1960s) is equal parts fashion and fantasy, a concoction that combines both the department's retro-candy product selection and fashion-driven branding efforts of Marshall Field's itself. The identity creates a playful aesthetic that appeals to both children and Marshall Field's female core guests alike. The centerpiece of the store's interior was the ceiling, beneath which two large female figures floated. One figure was blowing a bubble-gum bubble and the other was opening a box of chocolates which appeared to rain down on the customers below.

Studio: Wink

Art Directors: Richard Boynton, Scott Thares

Designer: Richard Boynton

Client: Target

Client's Services: retail

Illustrator: Richard Boynton

Inks: two PMS for vitamins, minerals and miscellaneous, three PMS for herb labels

Printing Process: offset

Options Shown: one

"This is a packaging system for a Target-owned brand product line of dietary supplements," explains Thares. "The tone and feel needed to reflect the current big-picture direction of the Target pharmacy (where the supplements are sold), which was leaning toward an organic/holistic approach to pharmaceuticals and health maintenance. By nature, vitamins need to communicate a lot of information (and in multiple layers) with very limited real estate." Wink's solution was to "strip away any and all pretense (decoration) in favor of a straightforward organizational structure. With the emphasis isolated on content and hierarchy, the typography is therefore forced to carry the load. The finished product evokes a sense of a traditional apothecary mixed with a hint of modernity via its relatively bright color palette of accents," says Thares.

Studio: Wink

Art Directors: Scott Thares, Richard Boynton

Designer: Scott Thares

Client: Marshall Field's

Illustrator: Scott Thares

Inks: four-color process

Printing Process: offset, letterpress

Options Shown: three

Special Production Techniques: letterpress printing,
limited edition numbered boxes, limited
edition gift cards

"Marshall Field's [before the Macy's acquisition] teamed up with the Art Institute of Chicago to release a limited-edition run of collectible gift cards, featuring famous masterpieces from the Art Institute collection. We named the campaign Field's Flora, since most of the artwork selected from the Art Institute involved floral paintings," explains Thares. "Paper for the art card sleeves was selected to accommodate letterpress printing and give the impression that this may have been something pulled out of a grandmother's attic, like a vintage flower seed packet." A limited-edition numbered soap box that contained all four collectible gift cards was produced as a store incentive. "The soap box included a letterpressed card, which allowed the guest to personalize the box as a gift," says Thares. "In addition, a direct mail brochure was mailed out to announce the Field's Flora Art Card Campaign, as well as showcase new merchandise at Marshall Field's."

Studio: Wink

Art Directors: Scott Thares, Richard Boynton

Designer: Scott Thares

Client: Target and National Geographic

Client's Services: retail

Photographer: National Geographic photo archives

Illustrator: Scott Thares

Inks: four-color process

Printing Process: offset

Options Shown: three

"The assignment was to reinvent the educational toy program under the National Geographic brand name to be sold at Target stores exclusively," explains Thares. "The design needed to accompany the product categories (nature, science and geography) while taking into consideration the various packaging formats—hangtags, open packaging, window packaging and closed-box packaging. The packaging needed to be fresh, informational and fun while encompassing the brand personality of National Geographic," which it does in brilliant fashion.

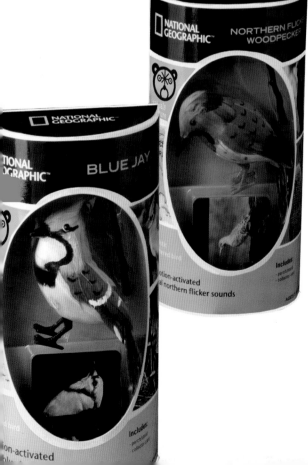

Studio: Sleep Op

Designer: Corianton Hale

Illustrator: Autumn Whitehurst

Client: Parenthetical Girls

Inks: four-color process, spot varnish

Printing Process: offset

Options Shown: one

For the second Parenthetical Girls record, "We've got this creepy, androgynous portraiture theme going ... " admits Corianton Hale. "The caricatures are of my friend Zac [the singer/songwriter], and it was his concept to put himself in bed with himself. We negotiated the conceptual implications of different body positions and facial expressions via Autumn Whitehurst and her spooky, realistic mannequin-esque illustration style." Hale raves that "the album itself is a gorgeous, heartbreaking, semiautobiographical piece of work, rich with powerful metaphors that I made efforts to represent throughout the design (cherry tree, keyhole, etc.) in spot varnish."

Studio: Sleep Op

Designer: Corianton Hale

Illustrator: Corianton Hale

Client: Tullycraft

Inks: four-color process offset

Options Shown: one

"This Tullycraft record was inspired (mostly) by Josef Albers and Reid Miles," says Hale. "The band already had a kitschy 1950s look to their albums, but this particular release marked a shift into much more mature subject matter and songwriting, so I wanted to cut the cute and really take the design a lot further, to a more serious level. Sean Tollefson [the singer/songwriter] and I collaborated on the creation of a ton of fake advertisements, many inspired by the classifieds sections of my 1960s *House Beautiful* magazines, but all responding specifically to song lyrics, or inside jokes between the band and our friends—so every ad is like a little puzzle to figure out. It's really dense. Of all my sleeves, it ranks highest in the 'toilet reading' category." he laughs.

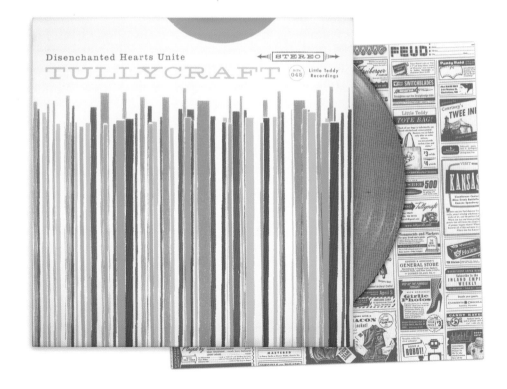

Studio: Sleep Op

Designer: Corianton Hale

Photographers: Richard Eselgroth III, Corianton Hale

Client: Daniel G. Harmann

Inks: four-color process offset

Options Shown: one

"The Daniel G. Harmann record began with the cloud photo that Dan (my roommate at the time) chose for the cover," says Hale. "I took the layout further by rummaging through my own box of Lomo photos and pulling out any that were mostly sky (there were a surprising amount). The album is called *The Lake Effect*, and I used this as a loose concept: working from the premise of the weather that comes down from the Great Lakes, the feel of the northern part of our country, and our relationship (as a country) to Canada." The look for the packaging was a good fit. "It all fit the moody, sparse sounds of the album perfectly," he says.

Studio: Sleep Op
Designer: Corianton Hale
Client: Corianton Hale
Inks: toner on copy paper
Options Shown: one

"Bulk Hulk was a party favor I made for my 27th birthday at this raunchy gay bar in my neighborhood," laughs Hale. "The party was called 'Beef Up!' and the flyers were designed to look like bodybuilding ads from mid-century men's magazines. I had a logo and buttons and drink specials—one was called the 'Protein Shake.' Come party time, I bought a grocery bag's worth of Vienna sausages, peeled off the labels, and fixed these new ones in their place." The label proclaims, "Easy to swallow sausage form!" Hale noticed that "by the end of the night, they were getting opened, tossed around and eaten. Occasionally, I'll see them in friends' pantries or on windowsills."

Turner Duckworth London, San Francisco

Number of employees: 15
Location: London, San Francisco
First year of business: 1992

"I did one packaging project at college that was so bad, I drop-kicked it out the window," laughs David Turner. "After my first job, I went solo and the only client I was able to continue with from my former employer was Schweppes, so I did a lot of packaging for them. Then I went into partnership with Bruce, and he's a packaging design guru, so here we are." Simply put, but it downplays the impressive results Turner Duckworth has seen. Since partnering with Bruce Duckworth, the firm opened offices in both London and San Francisco and work collaboratively between the two. The use of the other studio to give a "no punches pulled" critique provides a unique opportunity that other firms cannot compete with. This strong relationship has evolved from the days of the two sharing ideas on the phone to becoming the very essence of how they approach each project.

Many of Turner Duckworth's projects are packaging assignments. "Packaging is an important part of the design mix for over half of our clients. It's often where we start," explains Turner. "It's truly useful to consumers in a way that most marketing isn't," he says.

This discipline is where the firm has become best known, which is all the more rewarding because, as Turner points out, you can't get away with high concept without functionality on the grocery shelf.

Turner also explains the complexity packaging can pose. "Packaging is particularly challenging because it presents a unique combination of functional, legal, economic and environmental challenges, and yet it has to not only inform, but also differentiate and persuade," he explains. "It can be very costly if you get it even slightly wrong. We once designed a package for Levi Strauss that featured a subtle image of the face of the clothing designer foiled onto uncoated stock. The effect was exactly the opposite of what we expected, and the designer looked disturbingly like a monkey. We did the honorable thing and wrote a big check for a reprint. We certainly learned our lesson."

It can also be a frustrating arena to do battle in. "Blind trust in focus groups" bedevil Turner and "because of the high capital investment cost, the packaging production industry moves very slowly," he explains. "Despite the global need to reduce waste, there is still a shortage of great looking, mass scale, affordable packaging solutions that are truly sustainable," Turner laments.

Keeping the offices surprisingly small given the global clients that garner the bulk of their services, the philosophy of having the proof in the results and not in long, company-branded PowerPoint presentations has served them well. The two Brits like the creative tension formed by the friendly competition between the offices and, in particular, the principals. Serving as sounding boards and critics, the two continue to push one another as hard as they push the boundaries of design in the marketplace.

Q. What would be your dream packaging job? It can be an existing product or something not yet created for retail ...
A. We're working on branding and packaging for a product that may well extend life expectancy significantly. That takes some beating.

Q. Do you still get excited when you see your design sitting on the shelf at a store?
A. Absolutely. Especially when I'm not expecting it.

Studio: Turner Duckworth

Art Directors: David Turner, Bruce Duckworth

Designer: Jonathan Warner

Client: The Coca-Cola Company

Client's Services: beverage company

Printing Process: flexography

Options Shown: numerous

How do you make a classic even better? "Over the years, Coke's visual identity had become cluttered and uninspiring, diluting the brand's iconic status," explains Turner. "We redesigned the can as part of a total identity overhaul, clarifying the design and using the latest printing techniques to produce a bright white and a rich red," which makes a marked difference in the look of the final product. Pulling away all of the trappings inherent in the beverage field allowed the product to stand out immediately on the shelf.

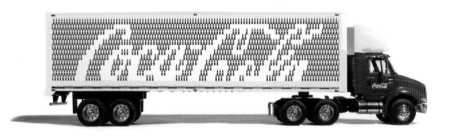

Studio: Turner Duckworth

Art Directors: David Turner, Bruce Duckworth

Designers: Sam Lachlan, Christian Eager

Client: Superdrug

Client's Services: drugstore

Photographer: Andy Grimshaw

Retouching: Peter Ruane

Inks: four-color process

"The objective of the redesign was to remind Superdrug shoppers of the myriad occasions on which they might need a wipe or two," says Turner. "Each pack has a different visual prompt of accidents waiting to happen, perfectly illustrating the point that it is not only parents with small children who should have a pack of wipes to hand. The designs show a bitten doughnut about to drip gloopy jam and an ice lolly starting to melt and create a sticky mess." The redesign is effective in a whimsical fashion.

Studio: Turner Duckworth

Art Directors: David Turner, Bruce Duckworth

Designer: David Turner

Illustrator: Tom Hennessey

Client: McKenzie River Corporation

Client's Services: beverage company

Inks: four-color process

Printing Process: flexography

Options Shown: numerous

"Our client simply said, 'Howling Monkey is the name. Have some fun with it.' So we did, creating a quirky brand from a bygone era for those partial to the odd beer," explains Turner. He is, however, selling short the firm's attention to detail, as they applied intricate illustrations and elements where others would have cut corners. The result is howlingly good.

Studio: Turner Duckworth

Art Directors: David Turner, Bruce Duckworth

Designers: Sam Lachlan, Sarah Moffat (vegetables)

Client: Waitrose

Client's Services: supermarket

Photographers: (spices and vegetables) Andy Grimshaw, (cat food) Steve Hoskins

Retouching: (all) Reuben James, (cat food and vegetables) Peter Ruane

Inks: various

Printing Process: offset

Options Shown: numerous

"Waitrose planned to launch a range of authentic Indian cooking sauces, once they had found an Indian supplier of the product. That task completed, they turned to us to create a visual identity for the new range," explains Turner. "Our team found inspiration in the sight and aromas of India's famous spice markets, where spices are piled high in fragrant, colorful mounds. The photographed spices are those used in each sauce, supplied to us from the creators of the sauces. Typography and background colors are further used to support the authenticity of the product."

Turner says, "Waitrose briefed us to redesign their range of premium cat food. The range consists of individual cans and mixed variant multipacks of tempting fish and poultry recipes. The solution lies in the bird's eye view every cat owner knows and loves of their cat's face. As soon as 'Tiddles' hears [his] owner start opening a can, he's standing there looking adorably upward, just waiting for the dish to be placed on the floor beside him."

"Waitrose asked us to refresh their canned pasta, vegetable and pulses ranges. Store cupboard staples for most consumers, the ranges had not been looked at in entirety for a number of years, resulting in a fixture that had become confused and difficult to shop," says Turner. "Our solution focused on using the products themselves to create graphic panels of the products shot against complementary backgrounds that would allow the consumer to not only stock up on their favorites, but also find new ingredients, too. Typographic style was kept as simple as possible to further aid communication."

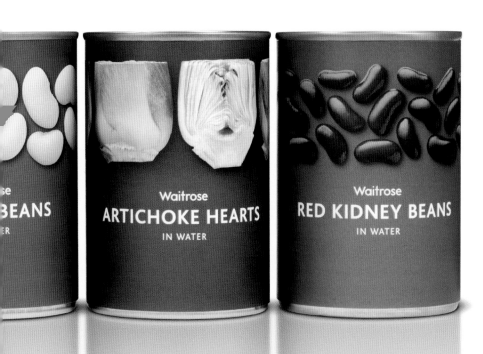

Studio: Turner Duckworth

Art Directors: David Turner, Bruce Duckworth

Designers: David Turner, Shawn Rosenberger,
Chris Garvey, Brittany Hull, Rachel Shaw

Client: Click Wine Group

Client's Services: winemaker

Illustrator: John Geary

Printing Process: offset

"This wine's name, Fat Bastard, describes the winemaker's opinion of its flavor," explains Turner. "The label was redesigned to communicate the high quality of the wine while celebrating its whimsical personality. A hippo has been a symbol for the brand since its inception. We brought him to life by redrawing him and sitting him on the label. Every detail was carefully considered, down to the wording of the product descriptions."

Studio: Turner Duckworth

Art Directors: David Turner, Bruce Duckworth

Designer: Shawn Rosenberger

Client: Click Wine Group

Client's Services: winemaker

Illustrator: Jonathan Warner

Printing Process: offset

Turner says, "Bootleg celebrates the creativity and style of a new generation of Italian winemakers by offering a collection of daring interpretations of classic Italian wines. Many Italian wine labels follow the usual formula of a hard-to-pronounce name and an illustration of the winery." Taking the name literally, Turner says, "We wanted to give a new twist to the tired cliché of the shape of Italy as a boot. The result is a sexy expression of contemporary Italian style that appears to wrap the bottle in skin-tight zippered leather."

As part of the redesign of Homebase's line of goods—more than 44,000 products—Turner Duckworth used a solution-based mode of thinking. For the line of cooking pans, the team created a brilliantly simple application of the food items that would be prepared on them via real life photography. Particularly striking is the shot of the egg in the frying pan.

Studio: Turner Duckworth

Art Directors: David Turner, Bruce Duckworth

Designers: Christian Eager, Paula Talford, Mike Harris, Charlotte Barres, Emma Thompson

Client: Homebase

Client's Services: hardware superstore

Photographers: Phil Cook, Steve Baxter, Andy Grimshaw

Retouching: Peter Ruane, Matt Kay, Josh Kitney

Inks: various

Printing Process: offset

Options Shown: numerous

"Our brief from Homebase was to create a range of packaging that communicated the breadth of their range of lawn seeds," explains Turner. "Consumer research had identified a need for single-minded, benefit-led communication in an area of the store where self-selection can end in the wrong product being purchased, but not in Homebase. The design solution uses photographic imagery to highlight both the problem and solution using turf cut into shapes that consumers could identify with the needs of their lawn."

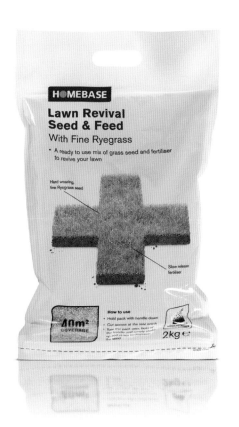

Allowing for the largest possible application of the color enclosed within, the firm's solution for Homebase paint cans not only makes the product readily apparent but shows the consumer what would normally be a hidden aspect of the interior. Turner refers to it as "the biggest possible paint swatch in the world!"

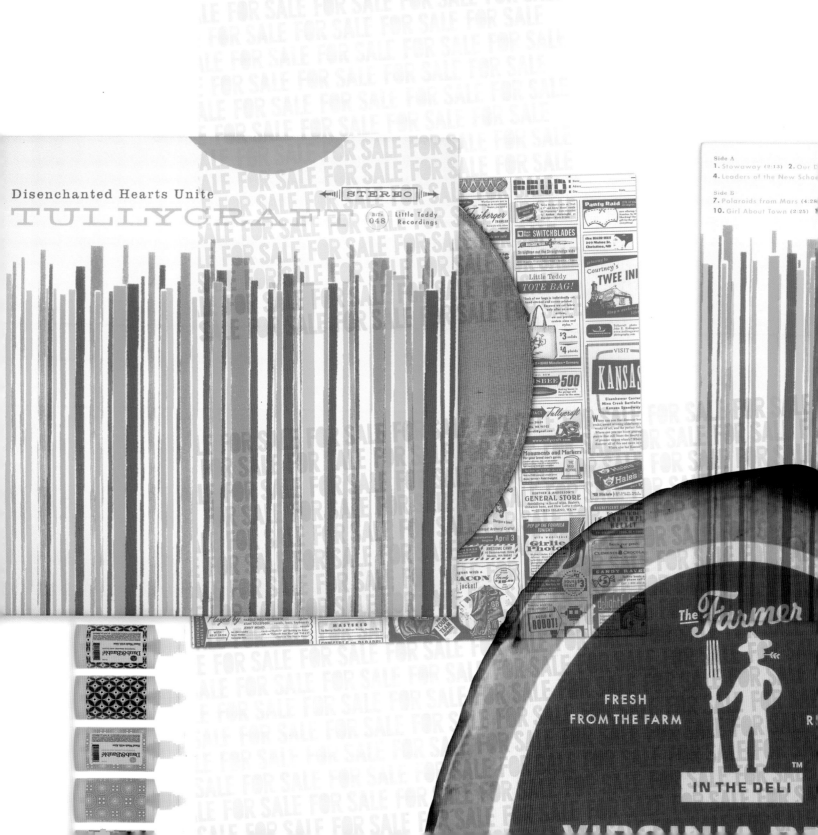

Studio: Terry Marks Design

Art Director: Terry Marks

Design: Terry Marks

Client: Glenn Mitsui (Flood)

Client's Services: digital image library

Illustrator: Terry Marks

Inks: two PMS colors

Printing Process: screen printing

Options Shown: one

Illustrator Glenn Mitsui was looking for a unique way to use his skills, according to Terry Marks. One day when Mitsui was attending church, he noted that the visuals left a great deal to be desired. He soon amassed thousands of illustrations specifically for use in worship services. According to Marks, "Knowing he had something, he approached us about creating some structure around [the church illustrations] to make them a viable marketable product." Marks branded the company as Flood and ultimately packaged it. He explains that they went back to the genesis of the name for the design: "We approached the design more symbolically and simply. The idea of water engendering baptism, renewal. It harkens to the heavens, and rain falling down upon humanity. Again, baptism and renewal."

Studio: 344 Design, LLC

Art Director: Stefan G. Bucher

Designer: Stefan G. Bucher

Client: Tarsem/Treetop Films

Client's Services: film production company

Photographers: Stephen Berkman, Ged Clarke, Steven Colover, Tarsem

Inks: four-color process

Printing Process: offset

Options Shown: three

Special Production Techniques: custom-made vinyl sleeve with a two-color silkscreen printing of a mask registered to the photo on the cover

Stefan Bucher exhaustively culled selections from more than eight thousand on-set shots for this 14" x 17" case-bound book of photography taken from Tarsem's new film *The Fall*. The book was created in order to promote the release of the film to potential distributors. During the design process, Bucher created a "mystique around the fantastic story and magical imagery." He adds that the book had to be hand-sewn "because at 14" x 17", it didn't fit on any machine."

Studio: Funnel

Designer: Eric Kass

Client: Funnel Paper Goods

Client's Services: premium paper goods

Copywriters: Eric Kass, Janet Harris

Inks: four-color process, spot stamp

Printing Process: offset with rubber stamp

Options Shown: numerous

"I was asked by one of my clients to create a gift paper for them to use as a holiday promotion," recounts Eric Kass. Excited by the opportunity, he in turn decided to design several patterns and create his own brand to market the paper. "It was a great chance to be my own client and craft every part of the brand," he says. He loved the design and writing portion, but fulfilling orders and the day-to-day grind gave him a "new appreciation for what my clients go through to bring their new products to market."

Studio: Funnel

Designer: Eric Kass

Client: The Original Pot-Tee Prize Grab Bag

Client's Services: potty training

Copywriters: Eric Kass, Janet Harris

Inks: four-color process, spot PMS

Printing Process: offset

Options Shown: numerous

"Potty training can be difficult and tedious," laments Kass. Using a package of stickers, a sticker chart, a certificate and a guidance brochure, he created "positive mementos of the event" to turn this process into a fun and treasured time. The stickers offer words of encouragement like "Good for Poo" and "Way to go, Squirt!" among other humorous words of praise.

Studio: Funnel

Designer: Eric Kass

Client: Maddy's Organic Meals

Client's Services: frozen organic baby food

Copywriters: Eric Kass, Dori Boneck

Inks: digital

Printing Process: digital

Options Shown: numerous

Inspired by the product itself, which Kass describes as "colorful, all-natural, frozen, farm-fresh cubes," the packaging result was "fun and sophisticated, healthy imagery." Incorporating an economical design for a start-up company which allowed orders to be filled by hand, he also provided "a brand image ready for the company's growing distribution."

Studio: Funnel

Designer: Eric Kass

Client: Films by Francesco

Client's Services: filmmaker

Photographer: Francesco

Inks: spot PMS

Printing Process: offset, engraving, silkscreen, letterpress

Options Shown: numerous

Packaging "beautifully shot and produced films that capture the events of our lives from a unique and honest perspective" proved to be a lot of production on Kass' end. Making a truly unique experience for the recipient of the piece, it utilizes four-color black-and-white images, engraved art on top of a green spot color, and a screen-printed DVD inserted into a gold engraved mailer. A system of labels, logos and bands allow Films by Francesco to create "their own variations on the package and other promotions," explains Kass.

Sub Pop Records Seattle

Number of employees: 2
Location: Seattle, WA
First year of business: 1988

An in-house design department is usually a tough place to make a name for yourself—as well as stay creative—over a long period of time. Jeff Kleinsmith, art director at Sub Pop Records, has managed to do both with equal tenacity (in his aw-shucks manner). During his fourteen years as the constant at the label, he's been joined by such wonderful designers as Hank Trotter, Jesse LeDoux and, currently, Dusty Summers. No matter who he is working with, though, he truly has the best interest of the company and the artists they represent at heart. As Kleinsmith is quick to remind me, "We work for the artists. If they are not happy with the packaging, then no one here is happy." The staff checks their egos, while gently adding guidance, as they deal with the most difficult clients. (For example, twenty-year-old musicians who think their abilities stretch from the musical to the visual.)

As 80 percent of their time is spent working on packaging, the staff can at least take solace in knowing that every project will be as different as each release will be. This is not a record label like Factory or Blue Note, where an overriding aesthetic takes precedence. Kleinsmith loves the process when "a package rolls out, and there are surprises around the corner—or folds, as the case may be. The cover tells a piece of the story, and as the package is opened, other parts are revealed."

However, he adds, "If you are breaking the story apart, it's a challenge to decide on where things go for that story to flow. How will the viewer read this when it is opened and unfolded? Sometimes, because I have spent so much time looking at the piece in a certain way, I lose sight of the other possibilities." He then passes around mock-ups and "if there is a difference in how the package is opened, unfolded or perceived, I will alter it to make it more obvious, or change it so that it could be opened in any way."

The label always wants to provide as much bang for the buck as possible—for both the artist and the buyer. This budget threshold can be viewed as a deterrent or, as LeDoux sees it, an opportunity. "With any constraint comes the challenge to turn a weakness into a strength. Tight budgets force you to be resourceful and think of unique ways to make a small budget look like a million bucks." You can really see what he means on the following pages. It's a quality LeDoux, Trotter and Summers have all adopted along with Kleinsmith.

Kleinsmith worries often about going too far. "Pulling back on the bells and whistles is tough. I feel compelled to add a diecut, or varnish, or an emboss because I can, but I pull back if it doesn't enhance the design. I try to keep those things at a minimum so that it doesn't come across as gimmicky." LeDoux adds that his favorite, as well as least favorite, part about beginning a package design is that the options are limitless. When they do decide to incorporate a special technique, they make sure it will have an impact and is fully integrated into the design.

Working with a single printer over the years has helped open up the possibilities as the gang at Sub Pop adjusts or creates templates. "If it's a standard package like a Digipak, then I just use the standard template—which can be modified with cutouts and embosses," says Kleinsmith. "If I choose to create my own package, then I am fairly involved with the design of it but leave the engineering to the manufacturer. They know more about things like creep or how much distance to add to a panel to allow for the fold based on the weight of paper I've chosen. That's, like, math or something," he laughs.

Q. What would be your dream packaging job? It can be an existing product or something not yet created for retail …
A. Kleinsmith: Nick Cave boxed set. LeDoux: A ten-foot-tall 3D cardboard display with many pockets, shelves and holes where a product with matching packaging can be placed. Maybe a big tree, where it has knotholes where packaging with squirrels and birds can be placed inside. I'm not sure what it would be selling, but after seeing the rad display, people would neeeed it!

Q. Do you still get excited when you see your design sitting on the shelf at a store?
A. Kleinsmith: Yes and no. If I'm happy with the design, then I'm proud, but if not, it can be like a sliver you'll never get out.

Studio: Sub Pop Records

Art Director: Jesse LeDoux

Designers: Thomas Campbell, Demetrie Tyler

Client: Sub Pop Records

Client's Services: record label

Printing Process: four-color process offset

Options Shown: five

Thomas Campbell says he originally "wanted to make a short film with the band Modest Mouse. I sent frontman Isaac Brock a package of stuff with films, doodles and other junk in it. When he got it he was like, 'What are these drawings?'" They could not seem to come together on a piece to work on, but soon Brock informed Campbell of his Ugly Casanova project and sent him the demos. Campbell fell in love and "made tons of drawings and some paintings" with his friend, Demetrie Tyler, "spending days trying to get it just right," and capture the mood of the music he had been living with. LeDoux was then charged with making sure everything worked in the packaging.

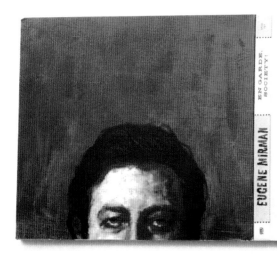
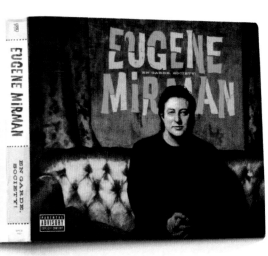

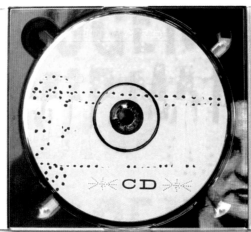

Studio: Sub Pop Records

Art Director: Jeff Kleinsmith

Designer: Jeff Kleinsmith

Client: Sub Pop Records

Client's Services: record label

Photographer: Brian Tamborello

Illustrator: Jon Daly

Inks: four-color process

Options Shown: one

"Eugene's previous record had a distinct Blue Note jazz record feel to it, which he liked," explains Kleinsmith. "He wanted to retain an 'older album' feel to the artwork. I felt that the Blue Note inspiration was a good starting point, but I wanted to shy away from being too reverential. I also wanted to shy away from an expected straight photo of the comedian on the cover. With that in mind, I hired this amazing artist named Jonathan Daly from Portland to reimagine a photo of Eugene as a loose oil painting, and I just took it from there."

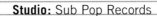

Studio: Sub Pop Records

Art Director: Jeff Kleinsmith

Designer: Jeff Kleinsmith

Client: Sub Pop Records

Client's Services: record label

Illustrator: Jeff Kleinsmith

Inks: four-color process, spot color

Printing Process: offset, thermography

Options Shown: one

"This is the third of the Sub Pop compilation triptych," says Kleinsmith. "The first was *Spanning the Globe for Profit*. Number two was called *Infecting the Galaxy One Planet at a Time. Patient Zero* shows how all of the efforts to span the globe and infect the galaxy went horribly wrong." He admits that "thermography changed the way I designed the piece. Initially, I wanted to do a foldout poster, but the size of the thermography heater was size-prohibitive, so I adapted accordingly."

"The band [Rogue Wave] had a very detailed vision for the cover involving a crazy dream, a dictator and a chessboard with animated chess pieces," explains Kleinsmith. "It was a decent concept but impossible for me to design. It would require an illustrator. They didn't want to go that route—they wanted something photographic. Instead of pushing it, I just went in my own direction, a direction that would ultimately become the cover."

Studio: Sub Pop Records

Art Director: Jeff Kleinsmith

Designer: Jeff Kleinsmith

Client: Sub Pop Records

Client's Services: record label

Illustrator: Jeff Kleinsmith

Inks: four-color process, dull varnish

Options Shown: one

Studio: Sub Pop Records

Art Director: Jeff Kleinsmith

Designer: Jeff Kleinsmith

Client: Sub Pop Records

Client's Services: record label

Illustrator: Jeff Kleinsmith

Inks: four-color process

Printing Process: offset

Options Shown: a ton

"This is a reissue of sorts, as Rogue Wave released a thousand copies of this album a year previous so when we signed the band, we decided to re-release it with new artwork," says Kleinsmith. "I had a long conversation with the band about the concept, and I set off to 'make it better.' I was very cocky about it initially because, frankly, the original release wasn't very well designed. I had the attitude that the band would pick whatever I came up with because it would be so much better—you know, because I'm a 'professional.' Wrong. Not only were none of them picked, they weren't very good. The band really pushed me to do something that fit their vision, so I came up with several more versions with a lighter, sunnier and happier feel to them."

Studio: Sub Pop Records

Art Director: Jeff Kleinsmith

Designer: Jeff Kleinsmith

Client: Sub Pop Records

Client's Services: record label

Illustrator: Al Columbia

Inks: four-color process

Printing Process: offset

"I have always been a big fan of [illustrator] Al Columbia's work. It's similar to Chris Ware but much darker, and with a very distinct and unique cinematic feel to it," says Kleinsmith. However, Sub Pop needed to take a gamble when Columbia wanted to try an entirely new style. "We loved what he does, but he came back with something totally different. The first version was of the same room on the current cover, but there is a photo of JFK sitting in a chair, very surreal and totally photographic." Legal stepped in, so he "chopped the face off and dropped a little alien cartoon character into the dark recesses of his head. That version was also rejected," he sighs. They soon arrived at the final cover, which adds an element of mystery so evident in the music. In the end, everyone was happier for taking the risk. "Al decided to work with photos for the first time ever for this record, and he nailed it," marvels Kleinsmith.

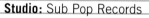

Studio: Sub Pop Records

Art Directors: Jeff Kleinsmith, Dustin Summers

Designers: Jeff Kleinsmith, Dustin Summers

Client: Sub Pop Records

Client's Services: record label

Illustrator: A Frames

Inks: four-color process on the interior package, one spot color (white) on the outer piece

Printing Process: offset

Options Shown: three

"The band was very specific with what they wanted, which was basically two square collages in the front and the back," says Kleinsmith. "We asked if we could show them a few ideas of our own while still using his artwork. We first showed the comp that would eventually be the final selection, but at first they were ambivalent. He liked it, but it was definitely not what he wanted. Slowly, he warmed to our layout, and by the end of the meeting he had chosen to go with this package." Getting it manufactured was another matter. "The outer piece was difficult because we wanted it to be a flood of black with a die cut. Underneath the die cut would be the black of the Digipak (so we had a kind of black-on-black look), but the issue there was that unless we used black paper, there would always be a white outline showing from the paper stock. So we went with black paper, which required us to print a spot white ink (four hits!) to achieve the look we wanted."

Studio: Sub Pop Records

Art Director: Jesse LeDoux

Designer: Jesse LeDoux

Client: Sub Pop Records

Client's Services: record label

Illustrator: Jesse LeDoux

Inks: four-color process

Printing Process: offset

Options Shown: one

Special Production Techniques: die cut and hand-folded so the booklet forms a pop-up chair

In the beginning of this project, LeDoux admits that "after going in several very different directions with the design, I was hitting dead end after dead end. I was completely frustrated!" Then, a breakthrough occurred. "I was doing the dishes while trying to figure out what I could do to make the package cool. I was about two-thirds done with the sink full of dishes, when I got the idea and immediately dried off my hands, grabbed a scrap piece of paper, and started cutting it up to see if the die cut I envisioned would work. And it did!"

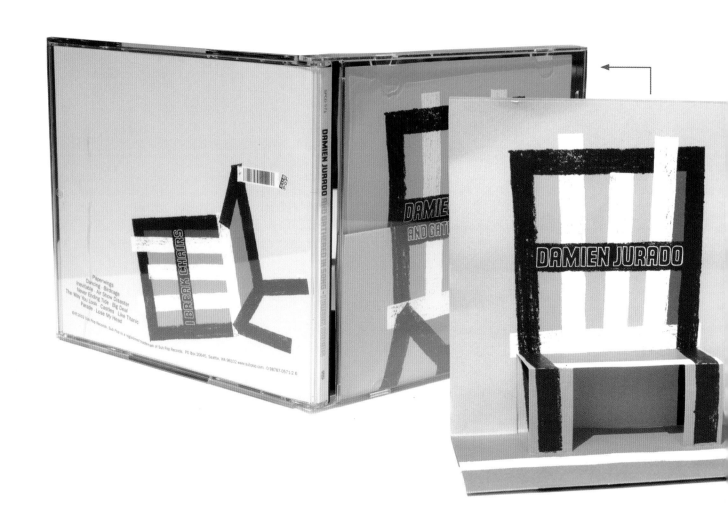

Studio: B.I.G. Ogilvy, New York

Executive Creative Director: Brian Collins

Creative Director: Weston Bingham

Designers: Helena Fruehauf, Iwona Waluk, Maja Blazejewska

Client: The Coca-Cola Company

Client's Services: beverage company

Inks: four inks

Printing Process: flexography

Options Shown: numerous

The Sprite slim can is a wonder to behold. A global soft drink adorned without a huge logo or any large, overbearing graphic? It seems impossible. Yet the B.I.G. team managed to remain "true to the brand," as Brian Collins puts it, while creating a consumer sensation. Focused on silhouettes of the Sprite drinking audience, the cans have a youthful nature and energy while not compromising the smart design. Refreshing.

Studio: B.I.G. Ogilvy, New York

Executive Creative Director: Brian Collins

Creative Director: Barry Deck

Designers: Hee Chun, Stella Lai

Client: The Coca-Cola Company

Client's Services: beverage company

Inks: four inks

Printing Process: flexography

Options Shown: numerous

Creating a holiday festive can for Coca-Cola, B.I.G. set out to "design a modernized Sundblom Santa against a background filled with unexpected yet relevant holiday imagery," explains Collins. The tough portion of a project like this is that "your audience is the general population, and you need to reach them directly from the point-of-purchase scenario," he explains.

Studio: B.I.G. Ogilvy, New York

Executive Creative Director: Brian Collins

Creative Directors: Weston Bingham, Barry Deck

Designers: Apirat Infahsaeng, Iwona Waluk, Stella Bugbee

Client: AT&T Wireless

Client's Services: wireless service

Inks: four-color process

Printing Process: flexography

Options Shown: numerous

Packaging the Ogo wireless device for AT&T, the B.I.G. team needed a design with wide appeal that also exhibited vibrancy. A brilliantly simple logo paired with dynamic colors banding across the metal tins brings the consumer in with a sense of comfort, yet embraces a modern flair, like few packaging designs can achieve.

Sterling Brands New York City

Number of employees: 85
Location: New York City, London, San Francisco, Singapore
First year of business: 1992

In college, Debbie Millman designed for the school paper and little magazines. While she had a passion for design, she didn't know where to focus it. After college, she fell into positions covering design, editing, traffic and everything in between: She was working hard but earning little. A break seemed to come with the formation of a new firm with the creative director from her last position. "All of a sudden we had a company, and then we had twenty people working for us. It was incredibly exciting. But ultimately, I didn't like the ethics of the company. And it was half mine! It's hard when you're working with one person because it's either you or them. Right now, I have two partners. So if you disagree on something philosophically, it becomes a round table. When you disagree with somebody philosophically and you only have one partner, it's an argument," she laments.

Financial rewards left Millman feeling empty, and she was adrift again until she landed a job at the prestigious Frankfurt Balkind firm. However, it was as a marketing director and not in creative services. Soaking up as much as she could, it was still apparent this was not her true calling. Lured by a headhunter to a branding consultancy, things started to come together. The move to Sterling would soon follow. "For the first time in my life, I found my niche. I have been working in branding ever since and am blissfully happy all of the time," she laughs.

The packaging business has changed over time, which is something the crew at Sterling embraces. "We have to recognize that brand and package design is not just about 'design.' There is no more 'mass market' in which to target a product. There is no one demographic picture of the planet," explains Debbie. "I have come to believe that the term 'brand design' ultimately undermines the job we do as brand consultants, marketers, designers and strategists. Brand design is not only about design. It is the perfect, meticulously crafted balance of cultural anthropology, behavioral psychology, commerce and creativity. It is about cultural anthropology because what we do in our culture—whether it is an obsession with reality television or weapons of mass destruction—this has a major impact on the brands around us. It is about psychology, because if we don't fundamentally understand the brain circuitry of our audience and really know what they are thinking—and why they are thinking it!—we will not be able to solicit their imagination. It is about commerce, because understanding the marketplace and the messaging impacts and influences perception. It is about creativity, because if we don't create a compelling package, then consumers won't notice it and buy it."

This pressure on a global scale creates unique challenges. "In some disciplines of design, it is absolutely critical and wonderful to 'see' a designer's voice—in a book design, poster design, magazine design or annual report design. But in package design, the consumer comes first, the product comes first, and the designer's visual signature should never, never be seen," Millman explains. "It is challenging to incorporate our thinking into the work, but not a particular design style. I think it is possible to incorporate a certain way of thinking into every assignment, but you are successful to varying degrees."

It also involves a ton of planning. "A great package design in isolation is easy. A great vision in isolation is easy. A great strategy in isolation is easy. It is having all three work seamlessly together that is the extraordinary and daunting—and most fulfilling—challenge," says Debbie.

It is also far from over in the design stage. "At Sterling, production is a discipline unto itself," she explains. "Our production process includes refinement and preparation of approved design files and artwork to ensure printability, using current industry standards. This stage is critical to the overall project process to ensure that all specifications, colors, information and graphic elements are reproducible accurately and consistently."

Q. What would be your dream packaging job? It can be an existing product or something not yet created for retail ...
A. Rebranding Britney.

Q. Do you still get excited when you see your design sitting on the shelf at a store?
A. Every single minute of every day. I am madly in love with this business and feel that my purpose at Sterling is to make the supermarket more beautiful.

Studio: Sterling Brands

Creative Director: Simon Lince

Designers: Gerard Rizzo, Carla Velasco

Client: Hain Celestial

Client's Services: food and beverage company

Illustrator: provided by client

Inks: four-color process, two spot colors

"Our key challenge was to create a new design for Celestial Seasonings that would create a brand block at shelf [level], without taking away the personality so intimately associated with the nostalgic brand," explains Debbie Millman. "Drawing from the historic word mark, our team explored a range of expressions, carefully refining inconsistencies, and finally envisioning an evolved, premium, sensual new logo that truly embodies the new essence. Coordinated color bands and consistent logo placement provide better blocking. The legendary artwork is presented in a cleaner format that focuses on flavor elements to increase taste appeal."

Studio: Sterling Brands

Creative Director: Simon Lince

Designers: Dan Walter, Stuart Whitworth,
Irina Ivanova, Andrew Markle

Client: PepsiCo

Client's Services: food and beverage company

Inks: four-color process, two spot colors
(black overprinted to add gradation in logo)

"Sterling's visual equity research showed that the 'straw in orange' (or SIO) was the key element in the orange juice category's sea of ubiquitous visual cues," says Debbie Millman. "The Tropicana team charged us with the task of leveraging the SIO equity to create a brand icon and to simplify the graphic architecture. This was achieved by developing a lockup of all elements, and the overlap of the straw in the last 'a' of Tropicana highlighted the importance of the SIO in all communications. Simplicity was achieved by making the SIO the hero of the package."

HEALTHY HEART

EXCELLENT
SOURCE OF
VITAMINS B6, B12
C & E WITH POTASSIUM & FOLATE

BEST IF USED
BY ABOVE DATE

Tropicana

PURE PREMIUM ®

100%
PURE ORANGE JUICE
WITH

LOW ACID

GREAT
TASTING
ORANGE JUICE
WITH LESS ACID

BEST IF USED
BY ABOVE DATE

Tropicana

PURE PREMIUM ®

100%
PURE LOW ACID ORANGE JUICE
WITH
VITAMINS A, C & CALCIUM
PASTEURIZED

SMART CHOICES
MADE EASY ®

Studio: Pentagram

Art Director: Michael Bierut

Designers: Jennifer Kinon, Kerrie Powell

Client: Saks Fifth Avenue

Client's Services: retail

Typographer: Joe Finocchiaro

Inks: two colors

Printing Process: flexography

Options Shown: numerous

"We understood quickly that this was more than a logo design project," explains Michael Bierut. "The current Saks logo had been in use since the mid-1990s, but had done little to create a profile for the brand, particularly as part of a gray-on-gray packaging program that was recessive, to say the least. Examining their history, we found the store had used literally dozens of logos since its founding. Many of these logos were variations on the same theme: cursive writing, sometimes casual, sometimes Spencerian. Saks was happy to emphasize its heritage, but it was even more eager to signal that it was looking to the future, a place of constant change and surprise, with a dedication to quality. The advantage of the program, deployed in black and white like the store's holiday 'snowflake' packaging, is that it creates recognizable consistency without sameness."

Studio: Stubborn Sideburn

Designer: Junichi Tsuneoka

Illustrator: Junichi Tsuneoka

Client: Stubborn Sideburn

Client's Services: design firm

Inks: four-color process

Printing Process: digital

Options Shown: one

"These pin badges are one of my promotional items," explains Junichi Tsuneoka. "They have been very handy, but I never had packaging for them. One day in one of my dreams, a guy with a long, white beard said, 'I like your button badges, but you need to pack 'em.' So I created the special package for them, and I don't have nightmares anymore."

Number of employees: 10
Location: Washington, DC
First year of business: 1997

fuszion Washington, DC

Rick Heffner was at a crossroads. He had worked at a premier design firm in Washington, DC, in its infancy, and then left to help form the in-house group that launched the template for broadcast branding at the Discovery Channel. He was exhausted by being involved in so many start-up situations, so starting his own firm seemed the furthest thing on his mind. Yet here he was getting office space and calling on clients. A decade later, he wouldn't have it any other way. Building a cadre of cable channels and entertainment clients, fuszion instantly stood out in the DC scene. Bringing John Foster into the fold a few years later, the firm branched out into advocacy and institutional work for nonprofits and museums. Foster had previously been in-house as well and the pair found that they understood the folks sitting across from them at the meeting table better than any other firm could.

Finding its home in historic Old Town Alexandria, on the Virgina side of Washington, DC, the studio is an anomoly in the DC market, with clients from all over the world, ranging from beverage giants to movie studios and every broadcast channel you can imagine. The firm enjoys the perspective available by not being embedded in the L.A. or New York scenes like so many of their competitors. "We grew up in the area and our families are here," says Heffner, "and we have worked hard to build a portfolio where the clients will come to us."

The sort of clients that find their way to the door are drawn in by the challenging solutions tailor made for each project. No cookie-cutter design here. "We have a need to keep our problem-solving skills sharp," explains Foster. "We don't do well working on the same thing again and again, but rather in finding that small little differential that changes the entire project." With that in mind, packaging projects often end up being the favored item to tackle. "We seem to learn or try five new things with every one," he laughs. "The entire studio works on them and we try to push the creative boundaries in every aspect, from design to the very mechanics of the piece."

Packaging covers about 25 percent of the studio's time, whether it be their prolific CD and DVD work or trying to move a billion cans of soda (the firm has worked for both Coke and Pepsi in the past including the famous Star Wars Pepsi series). "The challenge in this discipline for us has become the economics of the production," laments Foster. Heffner agrees as the firm "spent a full year perfecting customer relations with printers in Hong Kong" while re-packaging the entire line of XM satellite radios. They also agonized over the tooling to manufacture false plastic ice to cover a CD set of surf music housed in a real mini-cooler, only to see the budget change and make it unworkable at the last minute.

Still, with every challenge there is a lesson learned, and that's really what fuszion is all about. "If we haven't been able to take something away from a project that we can directly apply to something else we will work on that year—even if it is a color combination—then I feel like we have failed," says Heffner. Foster stresses that investing the time needed "to really try to *help* the client" is the key to their everyday success. "We have both been on the other side of that meeting table and we know what it takes to leave that room and make sure that the creative direction holds true through corporate review or the dreaded focus group. So we work hard to make sure we provide our clients with the tools they need to look good internally, and then we all look good in the end."

Q. What would be your dream packaging job? It can be an existing product or something not yet created for retail...
A. Heffner: A Styx retrospective.

Q. Do you still get excited when you see your design sitting on the shelf at a store?
A. Foster: I still geek out and catch myself looking for products on the shelves. The best is when folks you don't even know e-mail you photos of your work in a store. Then you know you have made a connection.

Studio: fuszion

Art Director: Rick Heffner

Designer: Phil Foss

Client: Discovery International

Client's Services: cable TV network

Inks: four-color process

Printing Process: silkscreen

Options Shown: six

"Over the years, what had previously been pretty involved marketing kits for Discovery, filled to the brim with inserts and one-sheets, had evolved into a CD-ROM," explains Heffner. "Moving the information into an interactive environment was easy enough, but then we realized we had a real challenge: The folks receiving these kits had high expectations for the visual experience, and our client wanted us to continue to get them excited about the programming." After a lot of brainstorming, the unique solution ended up being a custom water-filled pouch for the treacherous Alaskan king crabbing boat chronicles shown on *Deadliest Catch*.

Studio: fuszion

Designer: John Foster

Client: East Ghost West Ghost

Client's Services: music group

Inks: two spot colors

Printing Process: silkscreen

Options Shown: two

East Ghost West Ghost is the brilliantly named first instrumental solo project from musical maestro and indie rock legend Rob Christiansen. It is smart and complex—yet full of his simple melodies. I wanted to do something that complemented that aspect. Fighting off the urge to pursue my sketches of Casper-the-Ghost-like gang members, I made notes on what the music reminded me of and circled "racing." Taking advantage of staff members that bike to work, I shot the frame from a Mongoose dirt bike and the wheel from a touring racer. Thank goodness we have a variety of personalities in the shop, right down to what the gang drives in!

Studio: fuszion

Designer: John Foster

Client: Time-Life

Client's Services: record label

Inks: four-color process

Printing Process: offset

Options Shown: five

I love it when a client calls with a job and I just smile from ear to ear as they are explaining it. Such was the case with packaging a DVD jam-packed with highlights from Tom Jones' TV variety show at the height of his fame. When we received the still photos from the show, I saw a giant cut out of Tom smirking wiht the man himself in front of it, surrounded by go-go dancers. That's when I knew we had a winner (even though the photos had been badly handled over the years and needed a ton of work). We did have one regret: We wanted to show a fictional collection of panties Tom Jones had assembled over the years—women throw them at him on stage—behind the three discs inside, but ultimately his management nixed it as too sexy. Too sexy? For Tom Jones? Impossible!

Studio: fuszion

Designer: John Foster

Client: Chronicle Books

Client's Services: book publisher

Photographer: Eric Hansen

Inks: four-color process, two spot colors, UV

Printing Process: offset

Options Shown: eight

When you have beautiful photographs like these, you have to know when to just sit back and not overdesign the piece. Drawing a color palette directly from nature, these sets of journals and address books use the intense imagery to set the tone. To avoid "over-feminizing" the pieces, the firm instead set out to show the orchids in the best possible fashion, which meant using black as a surprising background color. The final result is both sophisticated and full of wide appeal. (This is the only thing I have ever done that my entire family has liked—I ended up giving them out as gifts, as I was getting barraged with requests.)

Studio: Teenbeat Grafika

Designer: Mark Robinson

Client: Teenbeat Records

Client's Services: record label

Photographer: Mark Robinson

Inks: four-color process, one PMS

Printing Process: offset

Options Shown: six

"I had been experimenting with photography of maps taken in the dark," explains Mark Robinson. "As Flin Flon always uses map imagery on their jackets, I thought it was a perfect fit for the Flin Flon's *Dixie* album. Since I'm also in the band, it was great not having a committee to approve the design (other than the two other band members who always appreciate my stuff). I always find I do my best work without someone else boxing me in."

Studio: Ashby Design

Art Director: Neal Ashby

Designer: Neal Ashby

Client: Thievery Corporation

Client's Services: musicians

Photographer: Daniel Cima

Illustrators: Neal Ashby, John Moore

Inks: two hits of custom red with black

Printing Process: offset

Options Shown: seventy-three

"Circles had become a motif on earlier Thievery album covers, if only by accident," explains Neal Ashby. "And it was again an accidental turn towards circles when Eric Hilton from Thievery showed me a Martin Sharpe poster with Bob Dylan on it. We both liked the trippy-ness of it before either one us realized it was composed of circles. That was the starting point and inspiration. We used circles in a very organic way on the cover, and then shifted to using those same circles as the DNA to systematically build photos on the interior of the package."

Studio: Ashby Design

Art Directors: Neal Ashby, Matthew Curry

Designers: Neal Ashby, Matthew Curry

Client: Thievery Corporation

Client's Services: musicians

Photographers/Illustrators: Neal Ashby, Matthew Curry

Inks: four-color process

Printing Process: offset with an emboss

Options Shown: forty-two

"Inspired by a shared appreciation of The Beatles' *Revolver* album cover by Klaus Voormann," explains Ashby, illustrator Matthew Curry and he set off to try their hand at a true collaboration for the package design of Thievery Corporation's *Versions*. Both served as illustrators and designers, using art from more than three hundred sources and "handing the storyline and digital files back and forth, over and over, until the lines between design and illustration were blurred," says Ashby.

Studio: Sussner Design Co.

Art Director: Derek Sussner

Designers: (bottles) Ralph Schrader, Derek Sussner, Brandon Van Liere, C.J. Marxer, Peet Fetsch; (golf) Brandon Van Liere, Brent Gale

Client: Reflections

Client's Services: printing company

Photographer: Bob Pearl

Copywriter: Jeff Mueller (Floating Head)

Inks: four-color process, spot PMS

Printing Process: offset

Options Shown: (bottle) one, (golf) six

"We've been working with Reflections for several years," explains Derek Sussner. "The relationship is so good and we work so well with them that 90 percent of the time, we show one concept and it's approved. They are really a dream client—almost too good to be true!" Working on the corporate identity down to their shipping cartons, Sussner knows the ins and outs of the company. "The good folks at Reflections have trusted us to stride right up to the edge—and peek over," he laughs. Designing promotions for them has been a challenge—whether it is finding tins for golf balls or tubes for champagne bottles or hand applying the labels.

Studio: Sussner Design Co.

Art Director: Derek Sussner

Designer: C.J. Marxer

Client: Montville Sales

Client's Services: shoe manufacturer

Photographer: Bob Pearl

Copywriter: John Arms

Inks: four-color process, spot PMS

Printing Process: offset

Options Shown: three

"Copywriter John Arms and I are outdoorsy guys and hunters (mostly water fowl)," says Sussner. "We brainstormed some concepts for the Tracker Tecs boots box, and what we liked most was the idea of using the box to say some fun hunting things—quips, facts and stories. The camouflage pattern we built is made of various animal shapes, and many of the compartments that hold type are hunting-related shapes—such as shotgun shells, duck calls, binoculars, etc."

Studio: Tim Gough

Designer: Tim Gough

Client: The Angels

Client's Services: music

Illustrator: Tim Gough

Inks: four spot PMS colors

Printing Process: silkscreen

Options Shown: one

Sometimes, working quickly with raw inspiration makes for the best solution. For The Angels, says Tim Gough, "this was done on the fly in a couple of hours." Capturing a sense of immediacy, "The image started as a tiny pencil thumbnail sketch, and I blew it up on a photocopier about a million times and left it as is. I felt the raw image represented the abrasive music these guys wrote," he says.

Number of employees: 2
Location: Minneapolis, MN
First year of business: 1991

Werner Design Werks Minneapolis

Some firms have a knack for making me smile when I see their work. Sharon Werner and Sarah Nelson Forss have continued to do so over the years as Werner Design Werks. Quirky, colorful and always on target, their mode of problem-solving is unique and engaging. Born from the initial design boom in Minneapolis when Joe Duffy assembled Werner (right out of college), Haley Johnson, Charles Spencer Anderson and others under one roof (but not for long), Werner finds inspiration in many of the found objects that the others do as well. What she does with them is where the difference lies. Patterns from thrift store finds take on new life, and whimsical illustrations spring forth. Sophisticated typography ties everything together, beckoning in clients, both big and small. Having that variety of clients is essential to keeping the design firm's chops sharp.

She was basically forced to open her own shop, since every time she interviewed at a firm, the principle would wonder why she wasn't opening her own firm, but Werner's days of doubt after leaving Duffy with no clients, prospects or money seem like another lifetime. Now the firm revels in its size, which allows them to be choosy about the kind of work they do and who they do it with. They establish a connection with their clients that few can match. Well-known in design circles for both her talent and her overall Midwestern "niceness," Werner has managed to leave a little piece of those qualities in so many of the firm's projects. It is that accessibility that comes through when you hold one of their products. Tactile and engaging, yet so very human, you find yourself drawn in by your memories and a desire to have some of those feelings rub off on you. Few designers today manage to connect in such a personal way with the consumer.

That she managed to find a like-minded soul in Nelson doubles the talent. It's no wonder clients as diverse and large as Nike, Chronicle, Nickelodeon and Target have called on the duo's talents. Twenty-five percent of the work may revolve around packaging, but half of that is from the wildly successful Mrs. Meyer's set of cleaning products. Werner makes sure to have as many different kinds of projects in the studio as possible, but their affinity for the packaging process comes through time and time again.

"I like the three-dimensional quality of packaging—holding it in your hands and turning it around, discovering the surprises," she says. "I also like to develop new forms, new methods of folding, exploiting the materials in new ways, seeing what it can do." Getting everyone involved in the process to feel the same way can present its challenges, though. "Convincing suppliers to have the same enthusiasm and drive to develop new forms, new methods of folding, exploiting the materials in new ways, seeing what it can do—all in a timely manner—is tough," she admits.

As project schedules have narrowed, she says, "Timing is always an issue: Anything that's custom or needs to be researched and tested takes a long time. It's like reinventing the wheel." She shakes her head, "I have great appreciation for unique packaging forms, not only for the creative aspect, but the determination it took on the designer's part to actually get it produced. We really appreciate the few suppliers that we work with that are as excited as we are to create something new." The clients appreciate Werner's determination to challenge the form as well.

Q. What would be your dream packaging job? It can be an existing product or something not yet created for retail …
A. Basically the next project is usually the one that has the potential to be the "dream" project.

Q. Do you still get excited when you see your design sitting on the shelf at a store?
A. Sure, but not as often as I used to. Unfortunately, the path of least resistance from a manufacturing standpoint has become the norm.

Studio: Werner Design Werks

Art Director: Sharon Werner

Designers: Sharon Werner, Sarah Nelson Forss

Client: Moët Hennessy

Client's Services: beverage company

Illustrator: Elvis Swift

Inks: one color, two color

Printing Process: offset, screen print

Options Shown: ten

"The project started out as a 'paid pitch' scenario with two other firms—one in Paris and one in London," explains Werner. "Fallon Brand Consulting introduced us to the yet unnamed project with the underlying positioning of alchemy, the mixing of elements to create something new." Pursuing the "elegant and classic crest and mixing it with the irreverent placement of the label, the raw beauty of Trinidad intermingles with the sophistication of France equals 10 Cane rum mixed with your favorite base—it's the redemption of the classic cocktail," she muses. "It takes approximately the juice of ten sugar canes to make one bottle of rum—no molasses here. The simple custom bottle is designed to be bartender-friendly, easy to grip and to pour while looking and feeling like the quintessential liquor bottle … with a twist. Mojitos anyone?"

Studio: Werner Design Werks

Art Director: Sharon Werner

Designers: Sharon Werner, Sarah Nelson Forss, Paul Sieka

Client: Mrs. Meyer's Clean Day

Client's Services: cleaning products

Illustrators: Sharon Werner, Sarah Nelson Forss

Inks: three spot colors

Printing Process: flexography

Options Shown: two

"When Monica Nassif approached us to work on this new brand of aromatherapeutic cleaning products, she already had a high-end brand in the market called Caldrea," explains Werner. "Her goal was to essentially rip Caldrea off and create a competing brand at a lesser price point. Genius! Knowing a bit about Monica and her background, we all decided that we should call it Mrs. Meyer's, after Monica's mother. Who wouldn't believe that an Iowa farm woman with nine kids and several pets would know how to clean? Since then, Monica's Midwestern mother has become the spokesperson for the brand. And whenever we question how something should look or be said, we channel Thelma—as well as our own Midwestern mothers—to find just the right tone for the brand. It's not out of the question to hear 'What would Thelma do?' And when in doubt, we call her."

Studio: Werner Design Werks

Art Director: Sharon Werner

Designers: Sarah Nelson Forss, Paul Sieka

Client: Cameo Beauty Lounge

Client's Services: beauty products

Inks: two color, three color

Printing Process: offset, engraved, foil stamped

Options Shown: three

Communicating a sexy, fun and sophisticated look, Werner says she worked with "the distortion properties of the liquid to magnify the sexy female drawing through the 'peephole.' This gave the entire brand a playful, fun quality the client was looking for. We wanted the bottle to levitate in the box, which was a bit tricky. The box needed to be scored at just the right depth so the box would hold its shape but still have a nice, clean fold. We love the contrast of the rough black chipboard and the sleek, shiny gold foil on the inside."

Studio: Werner Design Werks

Art Director: Sharon Werner

Designers: Sharon Werner, Sarah Nelson Forss

Client: Debby Bull

Client's Services: author

Inks: digital, one color

Printing Process: laser, letterpress

Options Shown: one

Collaborating with Debby Bull, author of *Blue Jelly: Love Lost and the Lessons of Canning*, to sell homemade jams and pickles at gift shops and book signings, Werner came up with colorful "Really Bad Jam" labels, which are "letterpress printed on pieces of vintage wallpaper." They then added philosophical messages, which were laser printed in the interest of budget and time. The playful result "allows customers to choose by flavor, wallpaper or message preference, and the author can change and add to the inspirational messages as often as she likes," explains Werner.

Studio: Werner Design Werks

Art Director: Sharon Werner

Designers: Sharon Werner, Sarah Nelson Forss

Client: Chris Huddleston, Rubyy

Client's Services: beverage company

Illustrator: Sarah Nelson Forss

Inks: four spot colors, matte

Printing Process: flexography on aluminum

Options Shown: six

The very mechanics of the production went a long way toward shaping the design for Rubyy, explains Werner. "The initial direction started with a clear PVC bottle, but due to the reaction of the liquid (with no chemical stabilizers) to the light over time, the client decided an aluminum bottle would be more shelf-stable for this blood orange energy drink. At this point, the entire visual direction changed." The firm originally wanted "a tall, thin bottle with a neck that didn't conjure up an image of a sport drink. We wanted a very matte black bottle, and the gray graphic is actually black light reactive, so it looks amazing in a club setting." Werner wanted to "play up the mysterious quality of blood oranges, dark on the inside, bright orange on the outside, so we chose to continue this mode of thinking—a dark bottle with light liquid. A typical orange drink would scream ORANGE, but this plays that down and lets you discover it as you taste the product," she explains.

Studio: Werner Design Werks

Art Director: Sharon Werner

Designers: Sharon Werner, Sarah Nelson Forss

Client: P. Puff Industries

Client's Services: clothing company

Inks: three spot colors

Printing Process: flexography

Options Shown: one

P. Puff Industries asked Werner to not only design the identity and packaging for a line of rubber belts, but also to design the graphics on the belts. Werner says, "We worked with the client to determine some trend directions for different demographic groups and went about designing a collection of products for kids, teens, men and women." They even worked with a plastics engineer "to develop the interior plastic piece that holds the belt in the 's' shape. There were some tricky tolerances for each width/length of belt. Our goal was to really highlight the belt, so the 's' shape ultimately becomes a significant element of the brand," explains Werner. "The rubber belts needed a protective package (oily fingers stain the belt) that would be dramatic and display the belt with lots of shelf appeal in the highly competitive gift market. The floating snaky 's' reinforces the name while showing off a sizable portion of the printed art on the belt and the buckle."

Studio: Werner Design Werks

Art Director: Sharon Werner

Designers: Sharon Werner, Sarah Nelson Forss

Client: Target

Client's Services: retail

Inks: four-color process

Printing Process: not printed

Options Shown: five

Coming up with a name and packaging for a Target kids' food brand, Werner presented "Let's Eat," a private label concept. The goal was to "create a packaging system that was fun for kids and communicated the nutritional attributes of the product for parents," she explains. Target needed the system to work across a broad range of kids' foods, "from cereal to frozen chicken nuggets." After a great deal of exploration, Werner was ultimately disappointed, as "Target decided that if they couldn't make the food better nutritionally than the other brands, they wouldn't proceed with a private brand."

FEED
me

GOLDEN HONEY bites

HONEY-SWEETENED CORN & OAT CEREAL

serving suggestion

NET WT 14 OZ (396g)

breakfast is the most important meal of the day

tongue tied

HERE'S **HOW**
IT WORKS:
1 Scratch your head
2 Fill in the blanks   2½ cut out the cards
3 Send it to someone who will appreciate your brilliance

ADD FRESH OR DRIED FRUIT TO YOUR CEREAL FOR ONE OF YOUR RECOMMENDED 5 DAILY SERVINGS OF FRUITS AND VEGETABLES

Milk not included... it gets the box wet
Spoon and bowl also not included

A GOOD SOURCE OF 10 ESSENTIAL VITAMINS AND MINERALS

breakfast IS THE MOST IMPORTANT MEAL OF THE DAY

FEED
me

APPLE 100% JuiCe

FROM CONCENTRATE WITH OTHER ADDED INGREDIENTS

10 POUCHES

FEED
me

CHiCKen NuggEts

LIGHTLY BREADED CHICKEN BREAST
(chopped and formed)

32 pieces or more

space shapes!

cook and serve

NET WT 24 OZ (1 LB 8 OZ) 680 g

Studio: Werner Design Werks

Art Director: Sharon Werner

Designers: Sharon Werner, Sarah Nelson Forss

Client: Target

Client's Services: retail

Inks: four-color process

Printing Process: not printed

Options Shown: five

"Feed Me" was also pursued as a private label concept and suffered the same fate as "Let's Eat" when Target could not confidently improve on the nutritional content.

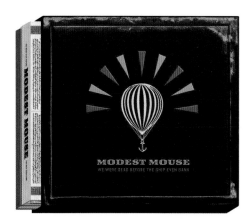

Studio: Decoder Ring Design Concern

Art Directors: Christian Helms, Isaac Brock, Naheed Simjee

Designers: Christian Helms, Geoff Peveto

Client: Epic/Sony BMG

Client's Services: record label

Illustrators: David Ellis, Casey Burns, Christian Helms

Inks: four-color process

Printing Process: offset

Options Shown: one

Special Production Techniques: emboss, deboss, three foils, various varnishes

"Decoder has worked with Isaac Brock [Modest Mouse's lead singer and architect of the band's unique aesthetic] a lot over the past few years," explains Geoff Peveto. "We were honored to be asked to collaborate on the new release." The catch? In true rock-and-roll fashion, there was about a week and a half to concept, design and deliver the project. "Christian flew out of Austin during the big ice storm of 2007 and into a freak Portland snowstorm to stay with Isaac for a few days and concept the album. After travel delays, his cab skidded into an oncoming car, and he was left to walk the last eight snowy blocks. Luckily, Isaac hiked down to help, and the two carried luggage and laptops through a deserted downtown Portland, stopping every few intersections to help push cars stuck in the snow." Intense brainstorming and interaction were followed by "a sea of proofs, a fortune in late-night phone calls and too much caffeine. The project was delivered to a stunned Epic Records. Less than a month later, the disc appeared on shelves, debuting at number one on the Billboard charts."

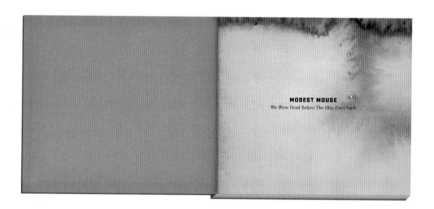

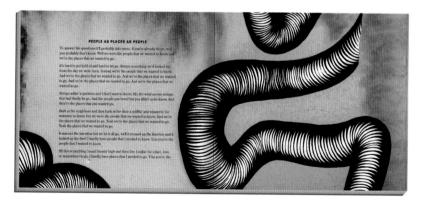

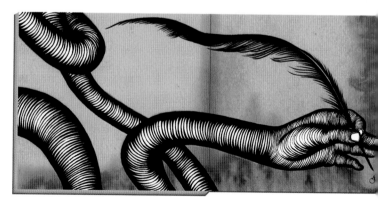

Art Chantry Tacoma

Number of employees: 1
Location: Tacoma, WA
First year of business: 1978

From his early days of shooting pool with Ted Bundy and witnessing the cresting of the trash rock scene in Tacoma, Washington, to becoming an icon of Seattle's design community—and the easiest name to throw out if you want a heated debate in that town—to moving to the slower pace of St. Louis, Art Chantry has finally come full circle: back home in Tacoma. He still has some of the intensity and nervous energy that informs so much of his work. He also has the sage-like viewpoint of a man who has seen so much take place in the design world. "I started out trying to do mainstream corporate work. That world included all sorts of packaging projects. I did odd items, like boxes for little rocks with google-eyes and mohawks glued to them marketed as 'punk rocks.' In that case, the sole criteria from the client was to make it look like a TR7 [a sports car of the era]," he laughs.

"The corporate guys back then were always crazier than the punk rockers—must have been all that cocaine, I guess," he muses. Yet it was with the punk rockers where he found his calling. "Years later, I moved on to doing LP and CD packaging for my friends in the music industry. The budget was much lower, and the creativity more challenging (no big budget to solve problems—just wit and brute labor). Strangely, nobody was interested in trying to make anything look like a TR7—go figure!"

The basic allure of packaging is not lost on Chantry. "My favorite part of doing packaging is opening up one of the shrink-wrapped finished pieces for the first time. It smells so toxic and wonderful, and seeing my work fresh for the first time is always a thrill. Nothing like it." Getting there isn't always easy, though. "Because our budgets were so low in the independent record industry, we had to imagine new ways of getting things done. For instance, if the fabrication of a record cover (trimming, folding and gluing) was too expensive, we'd simply get together a few friends and some beer, and fold and glue them ourselves one evening in front of the TV. If we wanted an elaborate die cut, we would simply use a pair of scissors. We solved a great many production problems by stepping back and doing things the old-fashioned way—ourselves."

"When we used most outside printing, we had to use mail-order print houses that would batch our projects into the runs of other larger record companies," he says. "Since these printers were far away, we never got to do a press check—so, we got real good at designing 'bombproof' projects that could go waaay wrong and still be acceptable without a reprint. Basically, we designed things that could color shift or go off register a great deal and still function. We had to plan disaster into the actual design in order to afford the manufacturing costs and release deadlines."

Chantry talks about the future of packaging: "Most packaging seems to have become cut and dried to the point that if you try to do anything that is not a standardized format, manufacturers will resist it (or overcharge outrageously to do it). Even something as simple as a PMS color will cause extreme reactions to change that are fraught with misery. Then, suggest printing on a piece of plastic rather than, say, cardboard and watch the fireworks start. I'm used to a nonstandard format, customized world," he laments. "The idea that simple change would be battled so venomously is always a surprise. However, since we now have super cheap labor in third-world countries available to us, it seems any wacky design idea is suddenly available for almost nothing!" Yet Art admits, "Ten years ago, I think better than half of my business was packaging design for record companies. However, the Internet distribution systems available now (downloading) and the adoption of computerized in-house design departments (cheap) by the record companies has almost eliminated the need for freelancers to do CD packaging design. The result is that now I imagine that less than 10 percent of my business is packaging design."

Q. What would be your dream packaging job? It can be an existing product or something not yet created for retail …
A. Well, it seems silly, but I always dreamed of doing a record cover for the Rolling Stones. It seems so silly now, because the Rolling Stones aren't the Rolling Stones any more. They seem to be a bunch of old wallets that mumble …

Q. Do you still get excited when you see your design sitting on the shelf at a store?
A. Yes, I do. I get a thrill when I encounter my work on the shelf. My work has been around long enough now, that lately, I've been finding my work in thrift stores and antique shops. I get even a bigger thrill out of that.

Studio: Art Chantry Design Co.

Art Director/Designer: Art Chantry

Client: Sabrina RockArena

Client's Services: record label

Inks: four-color process

Printing Process: offset

Options Shown: one

"This project, for the outrageous and extremely loud rock band Cookie, *Sweat-Soaked & Satisfied,* needed a huge amount of shock value and sheer attitude," explains Chantry. He certainly achieved it with the split face image that is arresting of the first order. "This was the first and only idea presented, and we all felt it hit the nail on the head."

Studio: Art Chantry Design Co.

Art Directors/Designers: Art Chantry, Jamie Sheehan

Client: The Criterion Collection

Client's Services: film

Inks: four-color process

Printing Process: offset

Options Shown: about ten

"This was a difficult project to execute," admits Chantry. "The Criterion Collection was attempting the produce one of their extraordinarily detailed packaging projects for the reissued remaster of this film noir classic film, *Le Cercle Rouge*. We designed a crisply beautiful and darkly moving image for the cover, got the OK and then produced the finished art. Then the owner of the actual copyright of the film, whom Criterion was leasing from, stepped in and wanted to completely change the design. Thus began a long back-and-forth attempt to just get a design acceptable to everyone involved. Somehow, we [Criterion and Art Chantry Design] managed to complete this project to everyone's satisfaction. It was tough getting there, though," he sighs.

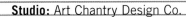

Studio: Art Chantry Design Co.

Art Director/Designer: Art Chantry

Client: Jason Frederick

Client's Services: musician

Inks: two-color

Printing Process: silkscreen

Options Shown: one

"This package actually began life as a poster for a rock concert [for another performer]," explains Chantry. "That poster was printed via silkscreen process by Jason Frederick. After a couple of years, Jason (also a musician) was self-releasing another CD project of his own work entitled *Last of the Cannibals* and asked if I could adapt that old poster image to a CD package. I agreed to do it, and this design was the result." Frederick continued his involvement by printing the packaging himself on his silkscreen press.

Studio: Art Chantry Design Co.

Art Directors/Designers: Art Chantry, Jamie Sheehan

Client: The Criterion Collection

Client's Services: film

Inks: four-color process

Printing Process: offset

Options Shown: about ten

"The reissue of Derek Jarman's early punk rock classic *Jubilee* was a bit of a challenge," admits Chantry. "How was I to create a new package for this punk film that was released at the height of early English punk style and not make it a simple copycat appearance or (even worse) an updated and now inappropriate version of punk design ideas?" he asked. "At first, I was a bit stumped what to do. This film was an odd and disjointed story line involving Queen Elizabeth and the alchemist John Dee trying to reinvent English culture by bringing down the British Empire. I had no idea how to depict this thing graphically." Viewing the film again made all the difference, he says. "In one scene in the early part of the film, Toyah and a few other crazy punks are leafing through a beautiful book of erotic photographs that have been nastily graffitied and disfigured with red marking pens. I took that idea and did the same to the cover and booklet of this film. I basically treated the design of this package as if it was that book of photographs—I attacked it and trashed it using processes that are pre-1978. I used analog copiers, old photos, masking tape, press type and marking pens to do this artwork," explains Chantry.

Studio: Art Chantry Design Co.

Art Director/Designer: Art Chantry

Client: Estrus Records

Client's Services: record label

Inks: four-color process

Printing Process: offset

Options Shown: one

The always inventive Chantry says the Midnight Evils' *Straight 'til Morning* CD package "is a good example of using a batch-printing 'mail-order' printer. We wanted a simple two-color design, but had to print it four-color (the red is a build of 100 percent yellow and 100 percent magenta) in order to be able to afford it. Surprisingly, it was more expensive to print it two-color (using a PMS color ink) than to simply 'fake' it in a four-color process press. Odd how things work out," laughs Chantry. For the design, he referenced the peculiar design notions of the King Novelty Company, a catalog mail order house that sold magic potions and voodoo charms back in the 1920s through the 1950s. "Whoever designed their amazingly colorful and crude label graphics was a primitive genius, and the packages are widely collected. With a name like Midnight Evils, we went for the obvious. We worked in a crudely produced red/black/white color scheme and illustration style like the catalog, and we would have printed it on old yellowed newsprint, too, if we could have afforded the expense of having the batch-printer we used re-machine their presses to accommodate it. Sometimes you have to go to war with the army you have, ya know?"

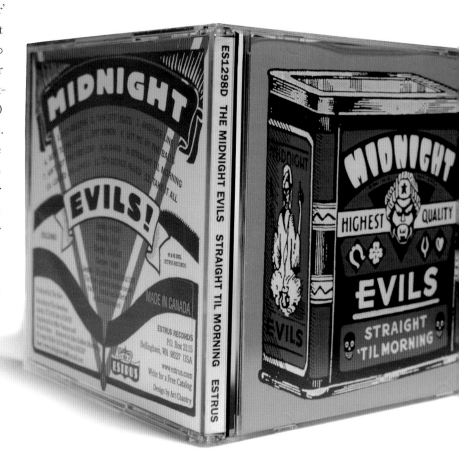

Studio: Jewboy Corporation

Art Director/Designer: Jewboy Corporation

Client: Sitra Ahra

Client's Services: book publisher

Photographer: Jewboy Corporation

Illustrator: Jewboy Corporation

Inks: four-color process

Printing Process: offset

Options Shown: numerous

You might argue that a set of books does not even remotely qualify for display in a book about packaging, but the mind-blowing design behind the Sitra Ahra collection from Jewboy takes the aesthetic value to another level, basically "packaging" the entire line of releases. If you don't agree with me, so be it. Sit back and enjoy the pretty pictures. "This book, *Pen Pencil Poison*, is about the thin difference between good and bad, with a devilish main character," explains Jewboy. "The image itself was one of my fastest drawings ever." Continuing the devilish theme, Jewboy mentions that "the writer asked me to put her picture in the back. She is very beautiful, but I hate the expected back sleeve picture so I trashed the image and put the barcode on her face, and she loved the result."

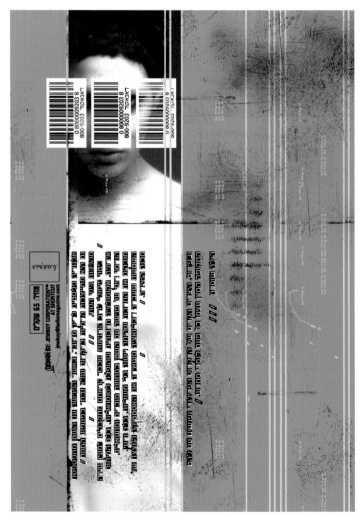

"The book *When Mussa Ran Off of Clonex* by Zvika Einhorn contains short stories and paragraphs with common subjects of death/drugs/city of Tel Aviv/depression/(failure of) love. Very optimistic!" laughs Jewboy. Wanting to establish a sense of surrender, he created an image of a naked boy socked with a self-destructive mood and antidepressant drugs. Jewboy says, "Still rather light, optimistic—almost funny." After the launch, the celebration took a wild turn. "The night involved a big mix of alcohol and pills and violence and a two-day disappearance. What can I say? It's impossible to not love and admire this guy, his talent and his craziness all at the same time," he sighs.

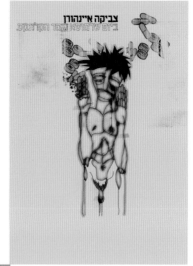 

1, 2, 3 Flood is a book of poems by Ori Shehter, ruminating on "love, hate and our existence. It's poetic, dramatic, sad … " explains Jewboy. "I tried to create something that resembled the feeling of suffocation I got reading the book." To do so, he says he used icons and symbols "to rebuild an image that would describe the feeling, but made it pinkish and light to keep it from the 'dark' zone it could so easily travel toward."

The first book by Shahar Saring, *The Long Way Down,* is a collection of "very personal stories by a young writer." Jewboy mentions that Saring "had lots of fears about the interpretation by people of the image of the penis on the cover," but he trusted his designer. "In the end, the public did not resent the image, but embraced it as the first edition was sold out!" he exclaims.

A poetry book about love, hate, sensuality, eroticism, self-hatred and failure … what's not to like about *Farewell Kit* by Shoshana Kirsh? As beautifully written as the text is, the design did not come easily. "This is one of the toughest projects I ever worked on," admits Jewboy. "I actually made four different covers with lots of crises and exhausting correspondence over the phone and mail in between. It took me ten months to finish this project, but it was worthwhile."

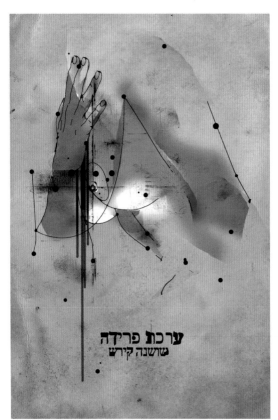

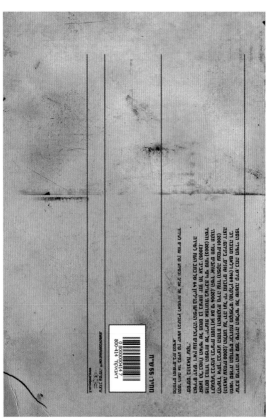

Finish is a collection of writings by Yuta San edited together by his friends and family after his suicide. "It was a hard process for them and I felt I needed to satisfy many voices—keep it respectful, yet as radical as the text and the man who wrote it," says Jewboy. "The outcome is a trip—basically, a business trip in a plane. No walls, no direction, just a small suitcase. It's a symbol of the decision Yuta made, and works with the vibe in his text. I think he would have liked the cover if he had seen it." The book launch was held at the cemetery near his grave.

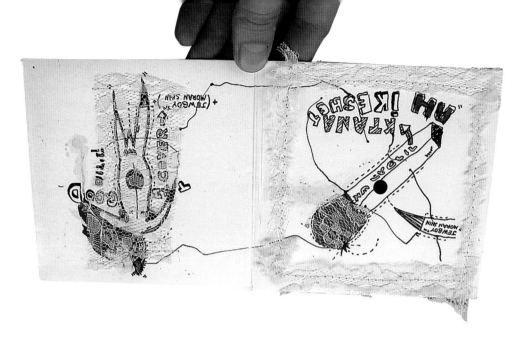

Studio: Jewboy Corporation

Art Director/Designer: Jewboy Corporation

Client: Teder Music

Client's Services: record label

Illustrator: Jewboy Corporation

Inks: handmade ink

Printing Process: sewing machine

Options Shown: one

"This was a crazy project, which included one hundred pieces of handmade art. Each one is unique and contains a different unofficial Gal and Maurin album," explains Jewboy. "This really was more of an experiment and a teaser/gimmick to create a buzz around Teder Music, followed by a big launch and a live performance by the artists."

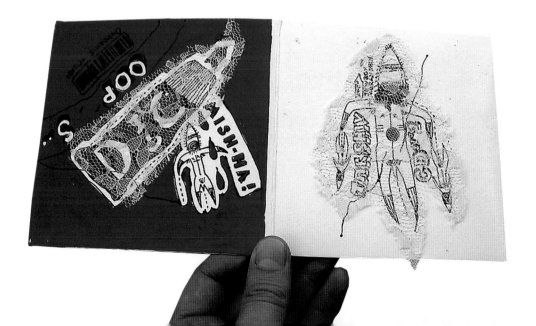

Studio: Jewboy Corporation

Art Director/Designer: Jewboy Corporation

Client: Teder Music

Client's Services: record label

Illustrator: Jewboy Corporation

Inks: one spot color

Printing Process: three rubber stamps

Options Shown: one

Working with Teder, Jewboy decided to "produce all the label's covers with the same technique: one spot color and three different rubber stamps. This would create a unique fingerprint for each cover, matching the creative perspective and musical vision of the label. Thus, for every production, we get to sit down and print 1,500 copies with three different stamps. It's nice with a beer on the side," he laughs. For Gal Tuschia's *RGB* DVD, he says he wanted to "compete with the experimental and colorful work inside as little as possible by making the cover typography-based." Using stains from printing and rubber stamps of the letters "RGB," he assembled the intriguing package before you.

Studio: Jewboy Corporation

Art Director/Designer: Jewboy Corporation

Client: Teder Music

Client's Services: record label

Illustrator: Jewboy Corporation

Inks: two spot colors

Printing Process: three rubber stamps

Options Shown: one

"Bonzai VL-1 by Maurin is a very repetitive electronic abstract and challenging record with a techno vibe," explains Jewboy. "I created a design made of connections between straight lines and dots. It is three huge rubber stamp blocks that are actually letters placed and aligned one over another. Lots of dirty hands with stains of ink that night," he laughs. After making the packaging, Jewboy says, "the guys from the label would go out with those huge stamps and stamp the city with those blocks" as a form of promotion.

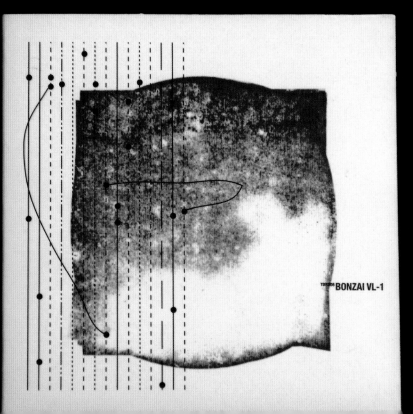

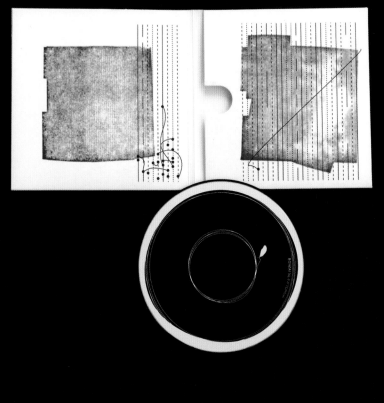

Number of employees: 6
Location: Palo Alto, CA
First year of business: 2006

non·object Palo Alto

"Non·object is a new kind of design firm—one that departs from the well-worn path of consulting, and embraces a new model focused on developing and licensing our own mix of branded and premium private label products and experiences," explains Branko Lukic. "We look beyond the object itself. Inside and out—we focus on the ethos that defines the being of an object. We create products that move you, that challenge conventional wisdom and embrace uncommon sense," he continues. Holding more than fifty patents, the firm is unique in the way it operates. Founded by a team filled with branding experience from working at some of the top agencies in the world, non·object both embraces what they have learned in those environs and reacts against it in its fresh thinking and insistence on creating products that make designers smile.

This firm eats, sleeps, dreams, and then wakes obsessed with packaging. By doing branding, as well as nuanced industrial design, they are the sole inclusion in this collection where you can say that they truly "design" every aspect of their products. Lukic describes starting the process as "looking at the object as I have never seen it before, like a child," and he then sets about to change the rules of how something is done. The result is that the team often pushes the accepted standards of design and manufacturing.

Since so few people are able to embrace this outlook, it can leave the firm in anguish. "The biggest challenge of all is others' inability to look at the world around us in a fresh new way. So many manufacturers are locked in their manufacturing principles and routines and are almost always trying to sell you what they have already produced for the last fifty years," Lukic laments. "In packaging, it takes us almost as much time—if not longer—to therapeutically convince our production partners that it is OK to change some radius or angles than it does to do the design. They easily become panicky when you move things around only because no one did it before—instead, I look at the challenge with a positive perspective and encourage anyone who will accept our challenge with enthusiasm, not fear," he grins.

The client can become an anchor for this adventurous spirit as well. "When clients have elaborate decision-making procedures, that almost always damages design intent," it bothers the firm, says Lukic. "A strong design idea or concept is actually very fragile, you move something just a little bit and then … puff … the magic is gone," he cautions.

Since their beginnings doing packaging design back in Belgrade, the capital of Serbia, where out of necessity—because not many other three-dimensional things were produced at that time—Lukic "quickly became a specialist, as we love to design something that people use every day, especially when it is connected to food or drink. Now non•object is growing into several directions—by its own intentions—and our plan is not to be solely specialized in packaging design. We are designing new experiences for businesses, whether for a Fortune 500 company, beverage startup or new technology company."

The pace of the design and manufacturing industry sometimes cannot keep up with the firm. "Recently, we wanted to do something that required more advanced laser printing technology, and process simply has not evolved fast enough for us to apply it in one of our designs. Printing processes have evolved really far in the past decade, but we would still like to see much more of fully recycled polymer-based paper, and the same would go for printing techniques," says Lukic.

I wonder if the industry will ever catch up to these forward-thinkers.

Q. What would be your dream packaging job? It can be an existing product or something not yet created for retail…
A. Two areas come to mind: un-bottled water and I would love to do a completely new perfume experience.

Q. Do you still get excited when you see your design sitting on the shelf at a store?
A. Absolutely!

Studio: non•object

Art Director: Branko Lukic

Designer: Suncica Lukic

Client: VODAVODA International Company

Client's Services: beverage company

Inks: three

Printing Process: flexography

Options Shown: one

"*Voda* means 'water' in the Serbian language," explains Lukic. "We call it VODAVODA because of that inspiration." Creating something to reflect the clean purity of the product, they also sought to be responsible in every aspect of the design. "We developed a square bottle that can fit more bottles per given volume than a common round bottle. This meant more bottles delivered to people for less money and energy."

VERTIKAL premium vodka. 700ml ℮, alc 40% vol.

✛ made with highest quality natural spring water vodavoda from banja vrujci source. bottled by si&si company product of serbia and montenegro.

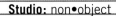

Studio: non•object

Art Director: Branko Lukic

Designer: Suncica Lukic

Client: Arteska International Company

Client's Services: beverage company

Inks: one ink

Printing Process: flexography

Options Shown: one

Starting the design process by "looking at bottle design today, we felt that the premium and ultra premium vodka beverage category deserved a more progressive design—one that would evoke emotion and push the limits further, while keeping in mind cost implications, engineering complexity and manufacturability," explains Lukic. "The question we asked ourselves in the beginning was: Can we make a bottle without a neck? That is where our journey started, and this is the result. The Vertikal Vodka, world's first neckless bottle," he smiles. "After its initial life as a product, the bottle was designed to be reused as an elegant vase."

Studio: non•object

Art Director: Branko Lukic

Designer: Suncica Lukic

Client: Arteska International Company

Client's Services: beverage company

Inks: four-color process

Printing Process: flexography

Options Shown: one

With more than twenty-six types of herb essences, Serbian liqueur Gorki List (which translates to 'Bitter Leaf') plays up those ingredients in its packaging. Green and covered in fauna, yet classy and sophisticated to suit the product's niche in the marketplace, its slightly bitter taste is also hinted at via the color scheme.

Studio: Nothing: Something: NY
Art Director: Kevin Landwehr
Designers: Kevin Landwehr, Devin Becker
Client: EDUN
Client's Services: clothing company
Photographer: Christy Bush
Illustrator: Kevin Devine
Inks: four-color process, spot PMS
Printing Process: offset, lasercut, foil stamp, thermal
Options Shown: one

Kevin Devine, the art director at EDUN—a socially conscious clothing company launched by Ali Hewson and Bono, along with designer Rogan Gregory—had reached the point where he was overbooked and could no longer produce the company catalog. "Of course, he wasn't going to turn this baby over to just anyone," remarks Kevin Landwehr. Nothing: Something: NY was on the job and up to the task. Wanting to hold to EDUN's notions of ethical fashion and organic clothing, they came up with an organic experience for the recipient. "This is one of the most complex laser cuts ever seen with no front side burn," explains Landwehr. "No printer wanted to touch this. The individual branches are purposefully designed to be thin and brittle, so that each book crumbles and breaks differently depending on handling. The more breakage occurs, the more realistic the night scene of dead branches and owls becomes."

Studio: Principle

Art Director: Pamela Zuccker

Designers: Pamela Zuccker, Allyson Lack

Client: Paddywax Candles

Client's Services: retail candles

Photographer: Kara Brennan

Illustrator: Allyson Lack

Inks: two PMS, acqueous

Printing Process: offset

Options Shown: numerous

"The Journey of the Bee was created as a tribute to the busy insect," explains Pamela Zuccker. "Each fragrance reflects a stop that the bee would make along its journey from the early blossoms of sweet clover to the raw honey in their hive." A "whimsical, gold-foiled flight pattern" is revealed on the glossy colored box when opened, and a matte black glass is adorned with a gold bee that is hand poured with a distinctive beeswax blend. This simplicity didn't come easy, though. "We found challenges in how the honeycomb pattern would wrap around the corners of the box," producing numerous dummy versions, says Zucker. "We also spent hours trying to figure out how to maximize the footprint of the gold-foil die (to maximize the budget)."

ROOM Nº

6

LOUNGE

CARDAMOM & TONKA BEAN

NET 26 OZ   **PADDYWAX**   100+ HOURS

Studio: Principle

Art Director: Pamela Zuccker

Designers: Pamela Zuccker, Allyson Lack

Client: Paddywax Candles

Client's Services: retail candles

Photographer: Kara Brennan

Illustrator: Allyson Lack

Inks: two PMS colors for each package

Printing Process: flexography

Options Shown: two

"The Home Collection was designed to appeal to interior decorators, offering the perfect neutrals, from basic black to canyon taupe," explains Zuccker. "Each exquisite fragrance unveils its unique character as you move from room to room." Packaged in a ribbed paper hatbox with matching grosgrain ribbons and a deco label, the paper was the key. "Mill-manufactured Estate Papers come in several different textured surface patterns and are predominantly used on wine labels to evoke a feel and look of the 'Old World,' and inks are easily absorbed into the surfaces, producing very muted colors," explains Zuccker, which finished off the look they had hoped to capture.

Studio: Principle

Art Director: Pamela Zuccker

Designer: Pamela Zuccker

Client: Paddywax Candles

Client's Services: retail candles

Photographer: David Lefler

Illustrator: Pamela Zuccker

Inks: four-color process, metallic PMS, acqueous

Printing Process: offset

Options Shown: numerous

For Paddywax's premier holiday collection, each glass is decorated with a delicate brocade pattern in precious metal palladium. "Taking a cue from fashion's metallic trend and luxurious European tapestries, we imprinted each glass with a rich ornamental silver brocade and repeated the same motif on a double-stacked custom setup box," explains Zuccker. "This elegant candle was designed sans brand name on the actual glass, allowing it to be a beautiful accent to your home decor for those that find name-dropping a bit conspicuous at the holiday table."

Production had its own challenges and research involved. "We wanted the brocade pattern to cover more of the transparent glass but were greeted with resistance from the glass company," Zuccker explains. "I had seen glasses with greater print coverage than what we were allowed. I never like the answer no without a good reason! We sought out other vendors to carry through our design but later learned that the U.S. had restrictions for glass vessels where certain paint products ventured too close to the lip of the glass. The glasses I had spotted on store shelves were foreign made and many of them violated the rule. It's important to pursue your design vision and not take no as an answer, but at the same time to protect your client from any possible hassles due to design or production."

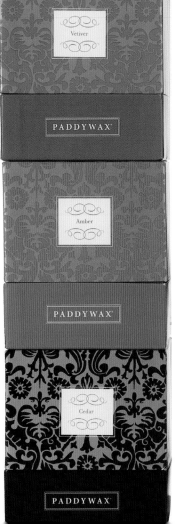
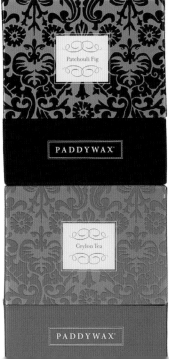

Studio: Principle

Art Director: Pamela Zuccker

Designer: Pamela Zuccker

Client: Paddywax Candles

Client's Services: retail candles

Photographer: David Lefler

Inks: four-color process

Printing Process: offset

Options Shown: numerous

Repackaging the Classic Collection was the first job Principle completed for Paddywax. "For Paddywax, packaging is the primary device for communicating the brand to consumers. It was with the Classic Collection that we began to focus on the brand attributes and move away from seasonal lines that did little to establish the Paddywax name," explains Zuccker. "We gathered feedback from Paddywax reps and retailers, which revealed that the Classic Collection's craft-colored packaging made it susceptible to being marketed as 'country,' not stylish." Using a "preppy-chic identity system," the firm set about establishing the main touchpoint for what would soon be a loyal consumer base.

Studio: Principle

Art Director: Pamela Zuccker

Designers: Pamela Zuccker, Jennifer Sukis

Client: Paddywax Candles

Client's Services: retail candles

Photographer: David Lefler

Illustrators: Pamela Zuccker, Jennifer Sukis

Inks: four-color process

Printing Process: offset

Options Shown: numerous

Zuccker says that "Paddywax wanted to launch a unique line of candles for spring that embodied the season: light, whimsical, feminine and fragrant. We designed the Jolie collection with dainty, vintage-inspired patterns in saturated spring hues—think Chinese paper lanterns, hummingbirds, pink pineapples and chandeliers." With this inspiration, Zuccker says that "each candle is hand-poured in matching Pantone colors into a smooth, flared glass, reminiscent of the always-fashionable A-line skirt. The four lively blends are named Pop, Fly, Bloom and Glow. Helping coin the names for this vibrant collection, we recommended punchy actions to set them apart from traditional floral and spice fragrances. Bright disk 'toppers' identify the fragrances and hold in the scent until burning."

Studio: Principle

Art Director: Pamela Zuccker

Designer: Pamela Zuccker

Client: Paddywax Candles

Client's Services: retail candles

Photographer: Kara Brennan

Illustrator: Pamela Zuccker

Inks: two PMS colors per package, acqueous

Printing Process: offset

Options Shown: two

"Inspired by the classic Greek key motif we recently spotted on table linens, tapestries and decorative pillows, the Adara Collection embraces this ancient graphic pattern on a full scale," explains Zuccker. "Spotting this trend in housewares and interior design, we knew it would have great impact on packaging that could serve as a gift wrap all in one. Just as important as our design strategy for each collection, we also bring to the table copywriting and a knack for naming. We pitched the name 'Adara' for its Greek name meaning 'beauty.'"

VERTIKAL premium vodka. 700ml ℮ 40% vol

TRYING TO REACH THE PAR 4 GR

3 18

REFLECTI

ETIQUETTE DEMA

SCIENTIFICALLY PROVEN TO CAUSE CONFIDENCE IN EVEN MEDIOCRE G
VISIT US AT WWW.REFLECTIONS PHP.COM
952 925 5100 FOR YOUR NEXT PUR

Play Better.

hacker - a very bad player.
mulligan - do-over, only in a friendly game
sandbagger - golfer who misleads others about
big dog - slang term for a driver, also known
hook - a shot that curves severely from rig
chunk - a golf shot in which the golfer
push - a ball that flies to the right of t

BETTER dAYS COMING NOW

Number of employees: 2
Location: Seattle, WA
First year of business: 2006

Invisible Creature Seattle

"Our love for art and design started in our early childhood," says Don Clark. "Our grandfather was an illustrator for NASA, and we always just wanted to 'do what Grandpa did.' In the mid-nineties, we started playing in bands. Those bands got signed, and we ended up meeting all kinds of people. I guess the rest is history," he laughs. Don makes it sound easy to connect one dot to the other, but the reality is more unusual. Helping form the design studio Asterisk, the Clark brothers began to stake out a reputation in music circles for their photo illustrations and in poster circles for their cartoon-inspired work. All the while, their band Demon Hunter was making a name of its own. With Ryan working as an art director for Tooth & Nail Records, all of these pursuits began to converge as the brothers started their own business. "The creature was born," as they like to say.

Virtually all of the work by the studio is for the music industry, and 90 percent is centered on packaging. To say that the Clarks have a passion for the form is an understatement. "There are so many reasons why I love packaging. I love the tangible aspect, I love the smell of the paper, I love holding it in my hands," says Don.

He also asserts that this integral part of the industry isn't fading away, as some have theorized. "I don't believe the propaganda that this will all be gone one day," he says. "Sure, things are going to change, but I hold true to the notion that there will still be some sort of music packaging out there. There are so many labels offering alternatives to the digital download, releasing vinyl and special packages. I hope that others will follow suit, and I pray that the kids still care about packaging—a necessary partner to the music."

This level of care and craft shows up immediately in the accomplished nature of their illustration work and their inventive packaging solutions. "When given the chance, we always like to push the boundaries in regard to CD packaging," admits Don. However, the best intentions can leave you wanting. "Sometimes we'll get proofs back that are completely off and leave us scratching our heads," he laments. "In one particular case, we had a die-cut circle knock out through the entire booklet, all the way to the stacking ring on the CD. We had countless phone meetings with the manufacturer on the details of the project. A one-inch circle knocked out through the booklet. Easy enough, right? Three weeks later, we get the booklet back with a one-inch *square* knocked out through the booklet. Imagine the looks on our faces."

They laugh about some of the other challenges. "We try to be as heavy-handed as possible, as we tend to get pretty passionate about what we do," says Don. "On occasion, a band might have a particular (bad) idea, and our hands can get tied the entire time. Needless to say, those projects tend to be our least favorite." They also long for a day when they aren't showcasing their work in tiny thumbnails on iTunes and still struggling with the printed piece. "Nine times out of ten, the design will always look better on the computer," Don says, shaking his head.

This dedication to their craft brings accolades to the studio from far and wide, as well as higher profile artists to their door. Their inventive, moody and complex photo illustrations have even graced Grammy-nominated packages for the past three years—Don jokes that it was his turn in 2007 after Ryan had the previous honors. The future looks bright for these self-proclaimed "tattooed mama's boys" indeed.

Q. What would be your dream packaging job? It can be an existing product or something not yet created for retail…
A. This year I was fortunate enough to design the Foo Fighters' new album. That was definitely in the "dream" category for me, and I had a blast working on it.

Q. Do you still get excited when you see your design sitting on the shelf at a store?
A. Absolutely. Sometimes we'll hit the record store and find all the packages we've done in one particular aisle at the store. It's overwhelming … we feel blessed that we have been able to make a career out of it.

Studio: Invisible Creature

Art Director: Don Clark

Designer: Don Clark

Client: Tooth & Nail Records

Client's Services: record label

Inks: four-color process

Printing Process: offset

Options Shown: one

"I pitched the idea to Jason Martin [of Starflyer 59] about doing something slightly 'organic' in nature, and that was to create the CD artwork with needles and thread—shoot it and add layers in post," explains Don. Using the typeface Perla as a reference, he says he "spelled out the band name and album title with red thread along needles stuck into foamboard. I shot each letter individually and created the rest of in Photoshop, adding the paper elements and textures, which were found at an estate sale from an elderly couple in west Seattle." However, it ended up being a tedious process. "The needle and thread aspect of the project ended up taking me a lot longer than originally thought. I spent almost an entire day—24 hours—creating the 'My Island' type," he laughs. "Thankfully, Jason gave me free reign, and the result was something I think both of us are proud of (and didn't have to be redone)."

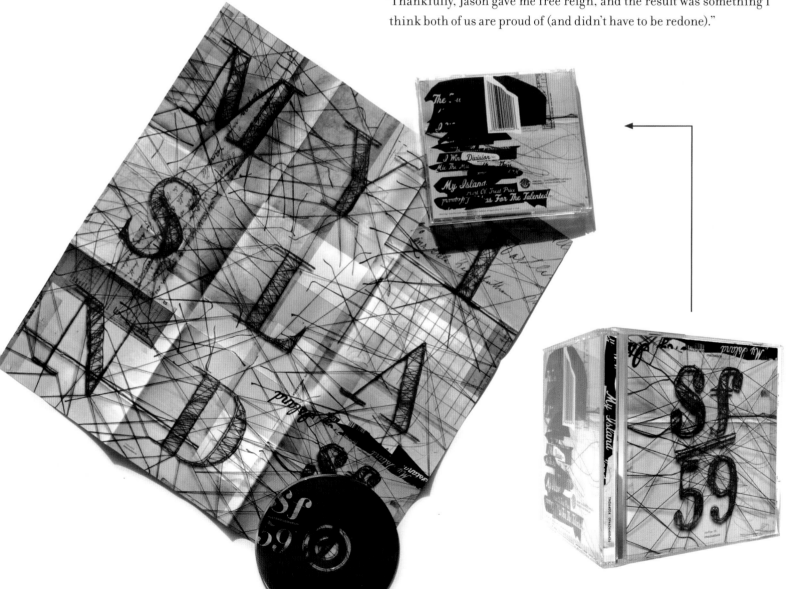

Studio: Invisible Creature

Art Director: Ryan Clark

Designer: Ryan Clark

Client: Tooth & Nail Records

Client's Services: record label

Illustrator: Ryan Clark

Inks: four-color process

Printing Process: offset

Options Shown: one

"As art director for the record label, I was approached to do the job with the idea that the band Far-Less was really interested in something different and unique" for their album *Everyone Is Out To Get Us*, explains Ryan. "I had just picked up some old horror movie magazines at a vintage store, and I thought this project would be a great place to use some of those old images. The album title just reminded me of something from a horror movie. It gave me a feeling of uneasiness. My idea was to have images of these screaming women from horror movies, but to leave out the reason for their terror. I thought it would be fun and interesting to leave that bit up to the viewer's imagination. The idea to use the TVs came to me as I thought of these old movies. I kept picturing someone renting these old movies and watching them at home." To accomplish this effect, Ryan says, "We had a three PMS color, clear, full-cover sticker placed on the jewel case, acting as an additional layer over the cover image, and also mixed paper stocks inside the booklet, using both coated and uncoated."

Studio: Invisible Creature

Art Director: Don Clark

Designer: Don Clark

Client: Trustkill Records

Client's Services: record label

Illustrator: Don Clark

Inks: four-color process

Printing Process: offset

Options Shown: one

"On Open Hand's first album, I did a similar styled die cut, so I wanted to do something just as cool (or cooler) for this album, and to keep the theme going," explains Don. "I came up with the concept of having these two hands reaching for each other, in what seemed to be a happy and positive environment. Once the viewer unfolds the package, it becomes apparent that this is not the case. One side clearly has contempt for the other," he laughs. "We had numerous phone meetings regarding the die and placement of the art. With the final product, the back inlay ended up being almost an entire eighth of an inch off. You can imagine how let down I was when we received the package in the mail. Most people don't notice, but it continues to haunt me every time I take a gander at it," he laments.

For Zao's *The Fear Is What Keeps Us Here,* Don "wanted to convey this sense of unexplainable comfort or loyalty to this figure, as well as random happenings around and under it." He developed the images to "define fear perfectly." Creating an "alien language that was only readable using a counterpart," Clark used the transparent vellum paper to continue a sense of fear and paranoia. A risky technique: "The vellum type pages didn't match up perfectly with the normal type pages—something I was afraid would happen, but somehow mentally dismissed," says Don. "This is the one major issue I had with the end result; however, I felt it wasn't a huge problem that you had to slightly move the pages to read it. I just told myself it was all part of the 'fear' concept," which it is creating an off-kilter viewing experience. It's nice when those happy accidents happen.

Studio:  Invisible Creature

Art Director: Don Clark

Designer: Don Clark

Client: Ferret Music

Client's Services: record label

Photographer: Jeff Gros

Inks: four-color process, spot PMS

Printing Process: offset

Options Shown: one

Studio: Invisible Creature

Art Director: Don Clark

Designer: Don Clark

Client: Tooth & Nail Records

Client's Services: record label

Photographer: Dave Hill, Jared Knudson

Inks: four-color process

Printing Process: offset

Options Shown: one

"One of my favorite designers is Stefan Sagmeister, and he was the originator (as far as I know) when it came to using colored jewel cases as an art form in CD packaging," explains Don. "In the blue jewel case, cyan becomes hidden, and anything with a yellow hue becomes more visible and darker. I used this 'hidden art' theme for the entire package, making certain aspects only visible under the jewel case and vice versa. Much respect to Mr. Sagmeister," he says. The band and their singer were not enthusiastic during the first pitch. "They are a pretty hands-on group, and they just didn't like the idea of trusting me on the end result. Showing them concepts via the Internet wasn't really making sense, either. I had explained to them in great detail what would be happening in the package, but, alas, they just didn't want to give up control. The entire process was an uphill battle," Clark says. "Once the band received the final package, they immediately called and almost apologized. They apparently were happy with the result. At one point, I specifically remember saying, 'This will end up in a design book, just trust me!' Slightly ironic," he laughs.

Studio: Octavio Martino

Art Director: Octavio Martino

Designers: Octavio Martino, Marcelo Schwander

Client: CCEC

Client's Services: arts center

Photographer: Octavio Martino

Inks: four-color process

Printing Process: offset

Options Shown: one

"Every year we design a new campaign for CCEC [Centro Cultural Espana Cordoba] that changes the way the center for the arts sends its programming pieces by mail each month," explains Octavio Martino. "Our studio created high-impact images on the covers, but the envelopes were almost standard shaped. So the following year, we decided to create something innovative in its shape, aside from its content. The result was this kaleidoscopic design that opens like a flower. The images in each envelope were not quirky, but rather a play on the name of the month."

Here you can see one of the standout selections from the series. It is making a play on the connection from harvested stock to final baked goods as you unfold to deconstruct the process.

Studio: Seripop

Art Directors: Yannick Desranleau, Chloe Lum

Designers: Yannick Desranleau, Chloe Lum

Client: Last Gang Records, DKD/Universal

Client's Services: Record label

Illustrators: Yannick Desranleau, Chloe Lum

Inks: four-color process, spot PMS, varnish

Printing Process: offset

Options Shown: one

"When our old buddy JFK from MSTRKRFT called us up about doing the art for *The Looks*, the first thing he did was praise the cover we had done for our own band, AIDS Wolf, and ask for something similar," explain Desranleau and Lum. "So we headed to the Salvation Army for collage material but kept the front cover more spare and minimal to reflect the house/techno contained within. Our concept was a pretty simple pun on the record title—the front cover has a woman with her eyes cut out. The eyes are die cut and allow the psychedelic patterns on the inner sleeve to show. The inner sleeve can be turned to create different views or ways of looking at the artwork."

All of the die cutting made for some intense production. "We took care to have the inner sleeves' designs match the die cuts of the jacket so you could place the sleeves in any position or angle, and the designs would 'match' (not showing some awkwardness, like text in the wrong spot, for instance)," they explain. The final result has garnered them a ton of attention and even won the pair a Juno (Canadian Grammy) Award.

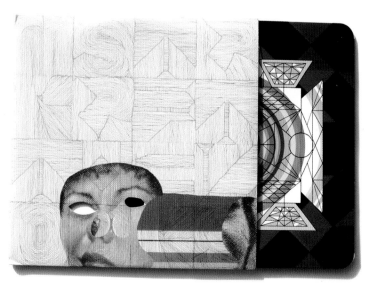

MSTRKRFT
THE LOOKS.

Side A
1. WORK ON YOU
2. EASY LOVE
Side B
3. SHE'S GOOD
   FOR BUSINESS
4. PARIS
Side C
5. THE LOOKS
6. STREET JUSTICE
Side D
7. BODYWORK
8. NEON KNIGHTS

Studio: Seripop

Art Directors: Yannick Desranleau, Chloe Lum

Designers: Yannick Desranleau, Chloe Lum

Client: Epitaph/Anti Records

Client's Services: record label

Illustrators: Yannick Desranleau, Chloe Lum

Inks: four-color process

Printing Process: offset

Options Shown: two

"We met Regan Farquhar, a.k.a. Busdriver, through mutual friends," explain Yannick and Chloe. "He knew a few folks we are pals with in the L.A. underground hip-hop scene and was touring with Islands, the band who our band was sharing a practice space with at the time. He arranged to meet up at our studio the night he was playing a show in Montreal. Immediately, we were impressed by him. First of all, the guy was very shy and dressed from head to toe in brown. His speech was lilting and would vary from fast to extremely slow, just like his rapping. Right away, we related as fellow weirdos." Playing off the dark lyrics and experimental music and the "Kill Your Employer" song, "it seemed to make perfect sense to go for an anarchist protest graphics vibe, hence the depressing-looking factory spewing smoke and the ground full of skulls," they explain.

Studio: Seripop

Art Directors: Yannick Desranleau, Chloe Lum

Designers: Yannick Desranleau, Chloe Lum

Client: Trend .

Client's Services: rock band

Illustrators: Yannick Desranleau, Chloe Lum

Inks: six spot PMS

Printing Process: screen printing

Options Shown: one

"Trend is a band from Berlin, and our designer friends Bongoût had designed their first project. About a year had passed from the time we were initially asked to do the project and when it actually came to completion. We even went to Berlin twice that year, but were always narrowly missing meeting the band," Desranleau and Lum remember.

Studio: Seripop

Art Directors: Yannick Desranleau, Chloe Lum

Designers: Yannick Desranleau, Chloe Lum

Client: Skin Graft Records, Lovepump United Records

Client's Services: record label

Illustrators: Yannick Desranleau, Chloe Lum

Inks: four-color process (two passes)

Printing Process: screen printing

Options Shown: two

Preparing to design their noise rock band's new disc, AIDS Wolf's *The Lovvers* LP and CD, Seripop knew they wanted the concept to follow the title of the record and the tarot card, and set out to assemble photography and band photos accordingly. Desranleau and Lum had two big hurdles to overcome. "First, finding the nudist camp photos wasn't as easy as we thought it would be. And then the printing! We printed an edition of 1,100 packages. We were on a very tight deadline because a) it took so long to do the art and b) we were heading out on tour. So we found ourselves in the studio the week between Christmas and New Year's. Each layer took about eleven hours to print with setup, reclaiming and dealing with the screen constantly drying out. We spent all of New Year's Eve printing and saw our studio mates leave around 10 P.M. and crawl back at 8 or 9 A.M. We decided to *never again* screen print such a large, ambitious run!"

Studio: Public Studio

Art Director: J. Gnewikow

Designer: J. Gnewikow

Client: Brushfire Recordings

Client's Services: record label

Illustrator: J. Gnewikow

Inks: four-color process

Printing Process: offset

Options Shown: three

"We were really trying to get away from a photo-driven direction for this package," explains Jason Gnewikow. "We wanted to bring a warmer, more personal feel to the art to reflect the introverted feel of the music and lyrics." Given free reign by the label, Gnewikow says he "had been playing around with watercolors mainly as a way to get away from the computer a little more, and it was really just for fun. I thought they had the feel I was looking for, and then I had the idea to come up with a surreal fantasy world, so we started experimenting with different vector shapes of plants and animals. And it just grew from there."

Studio: Public Studio

Art Director: J. Gnewikow

Designer: J. Gnewikow

Client: Flameshovel Records

Client's Services: record label

Illustrator: J. Gnewikow

Inks: four-color process, one spot color

Printing Process: offset

Options Shown: five

Having previously played in a band with some of the members of Maritime, Gnewikow was eager to work with them as a designer. "As a client, they're great to work for because they're very trusting and open to new ideas. We discussed what direction they wanted to go in for the artwork, and we both agreed that it would be interesting to do something a little darker for this record. The black ink spots mixed with the bright watercolor washes creates a nice balance between the lighter and darker aspects of the band," says Gnewikow.

Studio: Public Studio

Art Directors: J. Gnewikow

Designers: J. Gnewikow

Client: Jade Tree Records

Client's Services: record label

Illustrators: J. Gnewikow

Inks: two spot colors

Printing Process: offset

Options Shown: one

"This project was interesting because I believe they had someone doing the artwork before I came on board," remarks Gnewikow. "Snowden were really close to their deadline and asked me if I would be interested in taking a crack at the artwork. They had a tiny budget and no time. I had done this (laborious) illustration for a personal project but always thought it would make an interesting album package, so I showed them the original illustration and told them that they were welcome to use it, but there wouldn't be time for a lot of back and forth. The band and record label both loved it, so I worked all the type into the illustration, we made a few minor tweaks, and that was that. I think the turnaround was only a few days. A good example of why it's always good to be working on non-client projects."

Number of employees: 137
Location: Seattle, WA
First year of business: 1995

Starbucks Seattle

What emerged as simply good coffee from the sleepy city of Seattle has become the global leader in selling a lifestyle to the masses. The power of the product and the engaging wrapping it comes in has changed the way nearly everything is marketed. Starbucks has grown into a corporate leader while at the same time their hometown has shaken off the damp air and become an international destination. An in-house creative group was clearly needed. Starbucks began a studio internally in 1995, and now with well more than one hundred employees, they have not only matched the early creative brilliance of the brand—they have surpassed it. When brands take hold of their audience at this level, stale and safe executions can creep in. The crew at Starbucks casts that direction aside and blazes an exciting new trail of innovation.

It's telling in how far-reaching the aesthetics of the brand are that the studio only uses about 20 percent of their time to design packaging. Creative Director Stanley Hainsworth details how the work piles up with "retail promotions, retail environments, point-of-sale displays, advertising, store murals, print collateral, and a whole variety of communication materials." Anyone who has entered a Starbucks can see that they are a group of busy bees.

Packaging has a unique hold on the studio, though. "When you create anything that you can eventually hold in your hand—then feel, turn, smell, shake, open, consume, reuse, keep, give ... and then see it massed-out on grocery shelves—it's good," marvels Hainsworth, "especially if it's a product that you love and a design that you are really proud of. That's a good feeling." With the abundance of beautiful product coming off their desks, the staff must feel pretty nice every time they head to the local supermarket.

For those on the outside who might idealize the conditions for creativity they deal with on a daily basis, it is important to know that the Starbucks team faces the same hurdles as the rest of the design field. "The process of incorporating 'consumer insights' [focus groups] can be a challenge," admits Hainsworth. "We realize that the consumer holds precious information regarding the effectiveness of the visual communication of a design—but it's tough to maintain the original creative intent, or to innovate, when validation comes from a mass consumer point of view."

Once they clear a concept, it hardly stops there. The studio, Hainsworth explains, "always contributes sketches and identifies materials that we feel would best suit the brief" on the very industrial mechanics of the product. This is important, as the company as a whole strives for sustainable practices. "Managing all of the considerations and economics around print production—things like environmental sustainability considerations and maintaining the highest print quality for projects that are produced in very high quantities" is the stuff that keeps them up at night, admits Hainsworth.

With this insight into the daily workings of the in-house group, it makes it all the more stunning that they produce such breathtaking work. I have to admit that I don't drink coffee, yet I find myself wandering into Starbucks just to see what they are doing visually. Such is the power of the creative group.

Q. What would be your dream packaging job? It can be an existing product or something not yet created for retail ...
A. I think it would be for something that needs to possess the highest standards of environmentally sustainability, doesn't result in trash, is beautiful and tactile, and really contributes to a purpose beyond its own consumption.

Q. Do you still get excited when you see your design sitting on the shelf at a store?
A. How could we not? To work for months on a project and then you kind of forget about it as it makes its way slowly to the store. And then you walk in one day to your neighborhood grocer, and there is that old friend sitting on the shelf.

Studio: Starbucks

Creative Director: Stanley Hainsworth

Art Director: Kari Strand

Designers: John Close (Push Design), Jon Cannell, Fumi Watanabe

Illustrator: Fumi Watanabe

Photographer: Armstrong Studios

Writers: Heidi Watson, Thomas Prowell

Client: Starbucks Consumer Products Group

Client's Services: beverage company

Inks: four-color process, spot color, varnishes

Printing Process: offset

Options Shown: six

"Starbucks Drinking Chocolate is unique in the realm of chocolate and cocoa," explains Hainsworth. "The chocolate chunks combine with steaming milk to create a rich, velvety beverage reminiscent of the thick hot chocolate you might find in Italy. Our challenge was to design packaging that was equally unique, both communicating the immediate flavor appeal in the photography, but also the fun of nostalgic chocolate experiences. The special varnish and embossing touches create a distinctive pop on the shelf next to the other, more traditional hot chocolate products."

Studio: Starbucks

Creative Director: Stanley Hainsworth

Art Director: Steve Barrett

Designers: Steve Barrett, George Estrada

Writer: Stephanie Vandenack

Client: North American Coffee Partership

Client's Services: beverage company

Illustrator: George Estrada

Inks: five spot colors, including a special match semitransparent background color

Printing Process: offset, flexography

"Starbucks Iced Coffee is the most recent addition into the Starbucks ready-to-drink coffee portfolio," says Hainsworth. "The product is simple, delicious and even refreshing. The design attempts to convey the product's simple and straightforward coffee attributes with a minimum of elements and a no-nonsense name. The colored band families with the banding found on our core coffee packaging, while the silvery colored background represents a cold, refreshing coffee experience."

Studio: Starbucks

Creative Director: Stanley Hainsworth

Art Director: Kari Strand

Designers: Doug Keyes, Jeff Wilkson, Derek Shimizu, Margo Sepanski

Writer: Thomas Prowell

Client: Starbucks Consumer Products Group

Client's Services: beverage company

Photographer: Armstrong Studios

Illustrator: Kate Quinby

Inks: four-color process, spot colors, varnishes

Printing Process: offset lithography, flexography

Options Shown: thirty-five

"Our challenge was to take the current award-winning packaging that made Tazo a top-selling brand in the natural foods channel and evolve it to compete effectively in the cluttered mainstream grocery tea aisle, where Tazo's product assortment is considerably smaller," explains Hainsworth. "The new packaging leverages Tazo's original distinctive brand elements, bringing the color from the original filter bag packaging to the outside of the pack. To strengthen flavor appeal, photography highlights key ingredients. Exotic design touches and wit work together to captivate the consumer and suggest a tea experience like no other."

Studio: Starbucks

Creative Director: Stanley Hainsworth

Art Directors: Stanley Hainsworth, Toki Wolf

Designers: Jeff Wilkson, Fumi Watanabe

Writer: Stephanie Vandenack

Client: Starbucks Coffee Group

Client's Services: beverage company

Artist: Lane Twitchell

Illustrator: Jeff Wilkson

"For the Black Apron Exclusives line, the pinnacle of Starbucks whole bean offerings, Starbucks commissioned abstract artist Lane Twitchell to create artwork for a box that would be as special as the coffee it contains," says Hainsworth. "Starbucks selected Twitchell because his detailed designs reflect the painstaking care each farmer puts into growing these exclusive coffees. Art enthusiasts have discovered that there is more to Lane Twitchell's work than first meets the eye. His abstract paintings embedded with cut paper create complex, mirrored patterns filled with shapes visible only upon close examination. The artwork features intricate, hand-cut figures that reveal the human story behind these coffees."

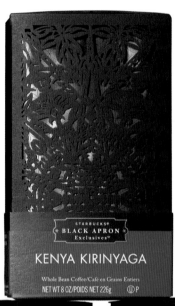

Studio: Willoughby Design Group

Creative Director: Ann Willoughby

Art Director: Zack Shubkagel

Designer: Stephanie Lee

Writers: Megan Semrick, Janette Crawford

Client: Feng

Client's Services: Asian fashion boutique

Inks: three spot colors

Printing Process: offset

Options Shown: three

"The Feng packaging system was designed to leave a lasting memory of the store experience," explains Ann Willoughby. "The shopping bags use the proprietary symbols and color palette in a cross-combination of bold pattern inside and out. The handles carry the "Essence of Feng" poem custom weaved in Chinese. Every inch of the bag was printed on, inside and out. With four bag sizes, we altered the pattern and color combination between the four sizes."

Each Feng gift box is topped with custom-designed wrapping paper, reminiscent of traditional Chinese wrapping customs. Willoughby created this wrapping paper pattern in full press sheet size and then cut it down to various sizes, so each piece has a unique look. All of the Feng gifts are tied with an antique-finished Feng coin to add an Eastern nostalgia. The interior flap features the four key Feng icons for antiques, home, fashion and tea with the Feng tagline "Look East." Now that's attention to detail!

Studio: 33rpm

Designer: Andrio Abero

Client: The Vera Project

Client's Services: nonprofit music and arts venue

Inks: four-color process

Printing Process: offset

Options Shown: one

Designing *Live from the Morning Alternative Vol. 2* for Seattle's nonprofit music and arts venue The Vera Project, designer Andrio Abero worked his strong typography into a seaside collection of iconic creatures. Compiling an eclectic mix of artists to help benefit the project's youth-empowering mission, Abero showcases them in an engaging package. This project continued to grow past this package, as it served as the inspiration for the the Bumbershoot campaign Abero would design soon after.

Studio: 33rpm

Designer: Andrio Abero

Client: Web of Mimickry

Client's Services: record label

Illustrator: Andrio Abero

Inks: four-color process

Printing Process: offset

Options Shown: one

Overlaying deep colors and graphic textures to create a deep wooded cover with the band name bleeding through the art, Abero set the tone for The Stares' *Spine to Sea*, and their folky, ethereal songwriting. Deep and drifting and organic, the use of trees seems particularly apt.

Studio: 33rpm

Designer: Andrio Abero

Client: Barsuk Records

Client's Services: record label

Illustrator: Andrio Abero

Inks: four-color process

Printing Process: offset

Options Shown: one

"I remember the first time I saw Aveo play," recalls Abero. "I was at a venue called The Paradox in Seattle and asked a random guy in the crowd if they've heard Aveo before. He replied 'no,' with a slight grin on his face. I said 'OK, well I heard they're amazing and the next big thing in Seattle, blah blah blah …' Ten minutes later, that random guy got on stage and blew me away. William of Aveo and the rest of the band were really fun to work with, always open to my ideas."

Studio: Kate Moross Design

Art Director: Kate Moross

Designer: Kate Moross

Client: Isomorphs

Client's Services: record label

Inks: four-color process

Printing Process: offset

Options Shown: one

For Cutting Pink with Knive's first release *Populuxxe* on her record label, Kate Moross worked using origami typography from patterns given to her by the band. Keeping each release to a limited edition, Moross says she is focused on "selling records as pieces of art, but not in a wanky way." With the goal of having the design process for each project be the result of an "intense partnership," her future output should continue in this amazing fashion.

BankerWessel <small>Stockholm</small>

Number of employees: 2
Location: Stockholm, Sweden
First year of business: 2002

Ida Wessel and Jonas Banker are sending their unique and colorful style of design and illustration out into the world from their studio in Stockholm—and the world is taking notice. No one has made so much from simple cut paper inspired shapes since Paul Rand. Seemingly new wave yet undeniably modern, they weave wonders from just a single letterform or doodle of a tiger. Where other studios layer on intricate imagery, BankerWessel simply cuts through the clutter with intensely bright color combinations and forms that have been honed down to their very essence. Having both studied at Konstfack in Stockholm, the pair went on to Otis (Banker) and Parsons and RISD (Wessel) in the U.S. before settling down in marriage. They returned home and now have two children to complement their creative collaboration.

When half of your projects as a small firm revolve around packaging, you obviously know what you are getting yourself into, yet selling concepts is a universally hard task. "I'd say my least favorite part of a job is when the client for some reason doesn't 'get' where you're going with your artwork," laments Banker. "One client once read too much into the graphics and thought that the buyers would be offended by the artwork. This type of lost communication doesn't happen at all that much, but it's very frustrating when it does," he admits.

However, the process of exploration gives the firm great pleasure. "My favorite part is if somehow in my work, I stumble upon something new and interesting that I haven't thought of or seen before," smiles Banker. This can enhance the work they do outside of packaging as well, because they always strive to "present the person or product in the most inventive and intriguing way possible."

It's that inventive streak that brings clients that strive for challenging solutions to their door. When Hefty label head John Hughes was looking for a visual foil, Hughes realized he tends to start his music by compiling "layers of elements that I can make work together, and from there, I strip it down. It seems that Jonas makes every attempt to begin simple and build from there ... or not build at all," he marvels. Hughes even went so far as to have Banker "design the faceplates for a series of custom rack panels I needed to have made for my modular synth. Since I stare at this synth for hours at a time, I wanted something inspiring to look at."

The entire process is a partnership for BankerWessel, as they view the folks they hand the files off to as essential to the final product and just as open to creative exploration. "I love it when the printer or the manufacturer of the box or the book has new techniques or new presses and capabilities or their own ideas," says Banker. "That's always a fun part, trying to find a new way of printing! Printing in new techniques or printing on the wrong side of the paper," he smiles.

Their playful solutions are matched by their wit and thirst for interaction. Perhaps my favorite transatlantic interview, the pair peppers conversation with Abba references and other Swedish icons. Banker said he would send me notes, with this caveat: "I even have a hard time writing and talking in my first language, which is Swedish. Trying to make sense and sounding cool in English is very difficult. Just take a look at Roxette, do you remember them?"

Q. What would be your dream packaging job? It can be an existing product or something not yet created for retail …
A. Right now, we're working on a new clothes line for babies called "tuut!" Great fun and very challenging to package our own product.

Q. Do you still get excited when you see your design sitting on the shelf at a store?
A. I love my job! So, yes!

Studio: BankerWessel

Designer: Jonas Banker

Client: Hefty Records

Client's Services: record label

Illustrator: Jonas Banker

Inks: four-color process

Printing Process: offset

Options Shown: three

Hefty Records "sent us music by Japanese musician Hirohito Ihara. We talked about making a pattern of how the experimental electronic music sounded. Putting the pattern on the CD disc and inside the booklet, we then wanted to create an image that would work with the name of the band—radicalfashion," explains Banker. Scrapping an abstract 1950s feel, Banker says, "We wanted the CD to feel contemporary and unique, so we finally came up with the image of a tiger looking 'right now, right here.'"

Studio: BankerWessel

Designer: Ida Wessel

Client: Arkitekturmuseet, Museum of Architecture

Client's Services: museum

Illustrator: Jonas Banker

Photographer: Niklas Dahlskog

Inks: four-color process

Printing Process: offset

Options Shown: one

Stadsplaner i Sverige is a book for the Museum of Architecture that BankerWessel "wanted to package with a playful approach to contrast with the town plan models inside," Banker reveals. "We wanted to play around with a kind of building stones and turn them into city blocks." The resulting illustration is striking in its graphic nature and sophistication.

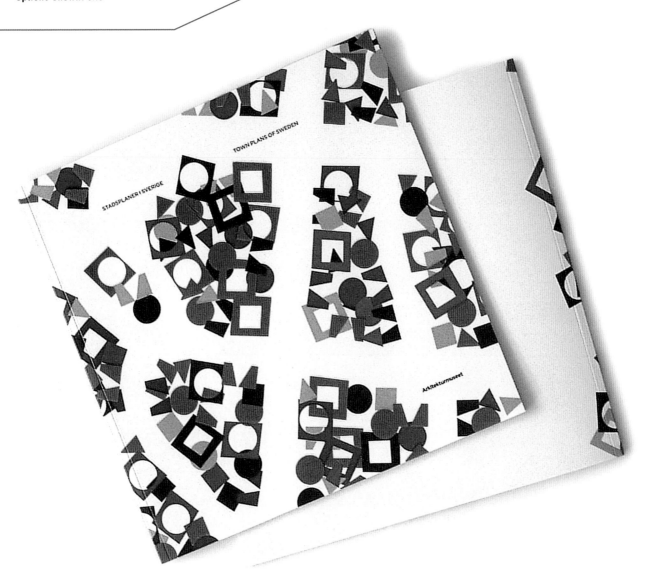

Studio: BankerWessel

Designer: Ida Wessel

Client: Gösta Wessel

Client's Services: artist

Illustrator: Gösta Wessel

Inks: one color

Printing Process: screen printing

Options Shown: one

"Artist Gösta Wessel made this limited-edition art piece," explains Banker. "It forms an optical illusion of a head with eyes always looking at you from any angle. We were asked to give the plastic art piece an interesting package to complement it." So Banker says the firm "made a simple cardboard box with the graphic face of the figure printed on the top of the box and the number of the edition printed on the back of the box."

Studio: BankerWessel

Designer: Jonas Banker

Client: Hefty Records

Client's Services: record label

Illustrator: Jonas Banker

Inks: four-color process

Printing Process: offset

Options Shown: one

"We always try to surprise ourselves and to have as much fun as possible with the artwork," says Banker. "John Hughes at Hefty Records contacted us, and we came up with the idea of illustrating each song on the album. The CD and the LP have slightly different layouts and completely different back illustrations. For the LP, we put all of the illustration credits on the hubs of the records." Banker muses, "In all of our work, there tend to be a lot of animals. This is based in our exercise of getting a job started by warming up by drawing animals, and birds especially. In this case, the funky birds found their place on the cover. Our work tends to be very intuitive and controlled at the same time, like a Herbie Hancock composition."

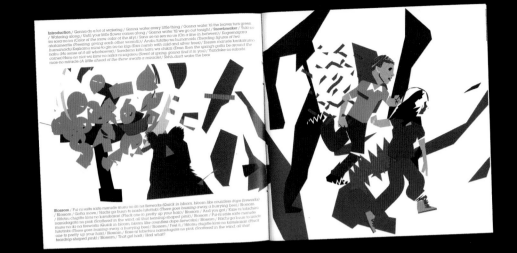

Introduction / Gonna do a lot of watering / Gonna water every little thing / Gonna water 'til the leaves turn green / Watering along / Until your little flower comes along / Gonna water 'til we go out tonight / **Snowbreaker** / Yuki no iro sora-no iro (Color of the snow color of the sky) / Sono ue-no sen no ue (On a line in between) / Kagenagara atatamearite (Freezing giving each other warmth) / Aruku futatsu-no humanoido (Treading figures of two humanoids) Ezakkaru mizu-to gin-no iro (Eau numb with cold and silver trees) / Teezen marude kankinuru nazku (No sense of it all whatsoever) / Soredemo kpto haru wa chikai (Even then the spring's gotta be around the corner) Hana-no nioi wo kimi no nakka ni sagasou (Scent of spring gonna find it in you) / Yukidoke no sukoshi mae-no miracle (A little ahead of the thaw awaits a miracle) / Shhh...don't wake the bear

Blossom / Fui-ni saite saite marude musu-no iin na fireworks (Quick in bloom, bloom like countless dope fireworks) / Blossom / Gotta move / Hachi ga buun to isode hitotbobi (There goes buzzing away a burrying bee) / Blossom / Hitotsu chigitte kimi no kamikazari (Pluck one to pretty up your hair) / Blossom / And you got / Kaze ni tabichiru namdagata-no pink (Scattered in the wind, all that teardrop-shaped pink) / Blossom / Fui-ni saite saite marude musu-no iin na fireworks (Quick in bloom, bloom like countless dope fireworks) / Blossom / Feel it / Hitotsu chigitte kimi-no kamikazari (Pluck one to pretty up your hair) / Blossom / Kaze ni tabichiru namdagata-no pink (Scattered in the wind, all that teardrop-shaped pink) / Blossom / That girl had / Had what?

01 INTRODUCTION 02 SNOWBREAKER
03 BLOSSOM 04 SOME WATER AND SUN
05 THE RAIN 06 A OH
07 WATERING 08 GLOOMY TOWN
09 ALL MY FRIENDS HAVE TO GO
10 MIZU 11 SEE YOU NEXT SPRING
12 EVERYTHING

SOME WATER AND SUN IS
JOHN HUGHES & SHIN TASAKI

Hefty Records
1658 N Milwaukee #287
Chicago, IL 60647 USA
www.heftyrecords.com
Ⓟ© Hefty Records 2005

SOME WATER AND SUN

ALL MY FRIENDS HAVE TO GO

Studio: BankerWessel

Designer: Jonas Banker

Client: Hefty Records

Client's Services: record label

Illustrator: Jonas Banker

Inks: two colors

Printing Process: offset

Options Shown: one

Supervise This is a compilation of different artists on Hefty Records. BankerWessel was charged with "coming up with a pattern that would almost act as a logo for the label," explains Banker. Moving forward, the pattern can be applied to any number of items for the label, as well as be printed in an inexpensive two-color manner.

Hefty Records
400 N Racine Suite 104
Chicago, IL 60622
(312) 633-9100 p
(312) 633-9127 f

www.heftyrecords.com
www.deepwaterstart.com

TV & Film: Josh Babyar
josh.babyar@heftyrecords.com

Advertising & Video Games: Jon Schultz
jon.schultz@heftyrecords.com

SUPERVISE
THIS
A COLLECTION OF MUSIC
AVAILABLE FROM
HEFTY RECORDS &
DEEP WATER START

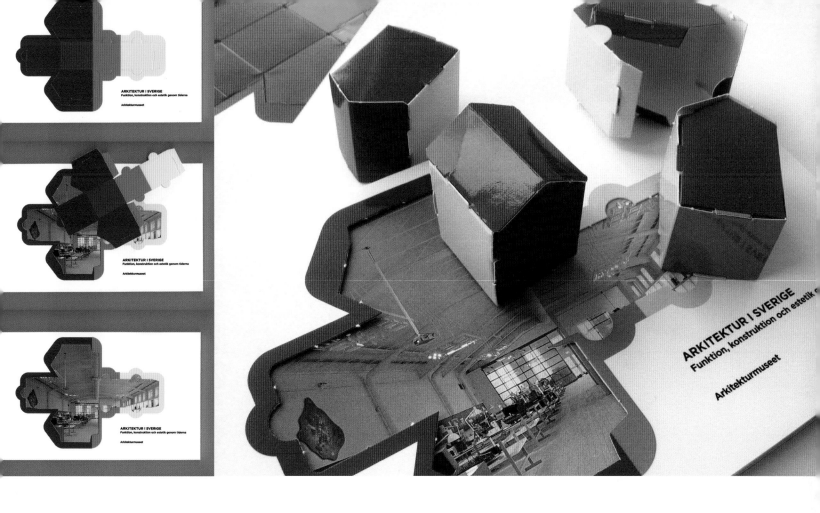

Studio: BankerWessel

Art Directors: Jonas Banker, Ida Wessel

Designer: Ida Wessel

Client: Arkitekturmuseet, Museum of Architecture

Client's Services: museum

Inks: four-color

Printing Process: offset

Options Shown: one

"*Arkitektur i Sverige* is the catalogue for the permanent collection at the Museum of Architecture in Stockholm, Sweden," explains Banker. "For the cover, we wanted to do something special and interactive to mirror the exhibition. We wanted to do something fun, playful and unusual. Architecture can be kind of stiff ... We came up with the idea of having the Swedish flag on the cover that would turn into a house if you pop out the paper by the cut line. The shape of the house is the three-dimensional version of the museum's two-dimensional logo. The museum didn't like the idea of the flag but liked the idea of having the cover turn into a house. They also liked the fact that the proportions of the catalogue were exactly 1:10 of the display tables in the exhibition."

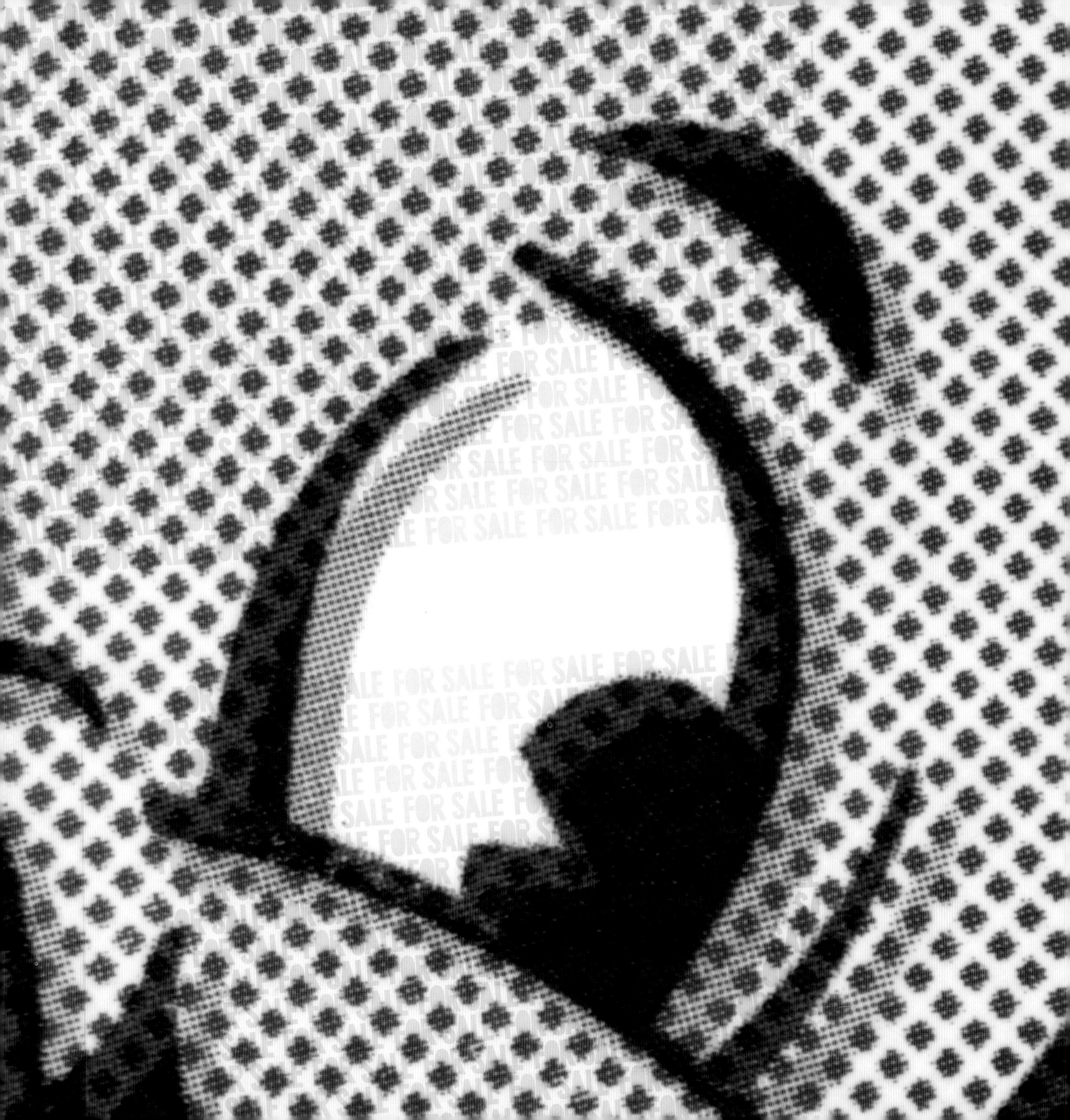
FOR SALE FOR SALE
FOR SALE FOR SALE

Studio: Aesthetic Apparatus

Art Director: Eric Skillman

Designers: Dan Ibarra, Michael Byzewski

Client: The Criterion Collection

Client's Services: publisher of historic, independent, art and foreign films

Inks: four-color process

Printing Process: offset

Options Shown: four

"The director George Franju succeeded in making an insanely creepy film years ahead of its time," shudders Dan Ibarra. "Face transplants, attack dogs, surgery disasters. It was all very subtle but still very disturbing." Keeping that subtlety was key for Aesthetic Apparatus. "With the package, we attempted to allude to the utter creepiness by not giving too much away. Starting at the front cover and the portrait of the doctor's daughter, main characters and pivotal scenes are carefully obscured by a floating white mask throughout the package and the DVD menu," explains Ibarra.

Studio: Aesthetic Apparatus

Art Director: Sarah Habibi

Designers: Dan Ibarra, Michael Byzewski

Client: The Criterion Collection

Client's Services: publisher of historic, independent, art and foreign films

Inks: four-color process

Printing Process: offset

Options Shown: four

"*If...* is the story of some English boarding school friends, who led by Malcolm McDowell [in one of his first film roles], wage anarchy on the school," explains Ibarra. "The film comes to a fairly violent end, which much of the original promotional materials for the film illustrated when *If...* was first released. It was obvious to us that to give away the finale before the viewer has even seen the film was pointless," he says. "Since McDowell is the lead protagonist and this is such a groundbreaking film in regard to his acting career, we chose to focus on his character for most of the packaging."

Studio: Studio Boot

Art Directors: Edwin Vollebergh, Petra Janssen

Designer: Edwin Vollebergh

Client: Design on Stock/Roderick Vos

Client's Services: furniture manufacturer

Photographer: Frank Tielemans

Illustrator: Studio Boot

Inks: three spot colors

Printing Process: silkscreen

Options Shown: one

Studio Boot was assigned to create packaging for a beautiful table designed by Roderick Vos— one of the best Dutch designers of the moment. "We were looking for package that would not be thrown away, but something that would make people buy the product just to own the box," explains Edwin Vollebergh. "So the package had to be beautiful, but also had to communicate that there is something valuable inside." Studio Boot wanted to make that connection between the finish on the table and the box. Vollebergh says, "The silver is pouring over the edge and dripping alongside the box." Once opened, buyers are keeping the boxes for display and storage. "It's a hit," smiles Vollebergh.

Studio: Studio Boot

Art Directors: Edwin Vollebergh, Patrick van de Heijden

Designer: Edwin Vollebergh

Client: HomePlan Foundation

Client's Services: building houses for AIDS-orphans in South Africa

Illustrator: Studio Boot

Inks: two spot colors

Printing Process: silkscreen

Options Shown: one

No House Wine is a new South African wine brand created specifically to benefit the Dutch foundation HomePlan. "A percentage of the profit goes to build homes for South African AIDS orphans," explains Vollebergh. "The wine is a huge success in the Netherlands and has already raised enough money to build ten houses." The final piece is intended "to look handmade and rough. The materials chosen are common and inexpensive, therefore keeping the cost as low as possible so more money can be donated to the cause."

Studio: Burlesque of North America

Art Director: Wes Winship

Designers: Wes Winship, Adam Garcia

Client: Arcade Fire

Client's Services: rock band

Photographer: Wes Winship

Illustrator: Adam Garcia

Inks: three spot colors

Printing Process: silkscreen

Options Shown: one

Continuing a relationship with Arcade Fire, Wes Winship knew what he wanted to explore for a tour poster. "[Comic artist] Chris Ware's work had planted an interest in me in making paper toys. I had already explored this a little with a few earlier band posters. Their music can have a childlike quality to it, at times innocent and other times struggling with the loss of that innocence. I've tried to work that feeling into the work I've done for them, which made a paper toy idea fit right in," he explains. Based on an old Nabisco box top game, the Burlesque team set out to take the rough shape and turn it into a shadow box with the inside illustrated. Painstakingly working out the mechanics, they would not settle until they could put it together with just a set of scissors.

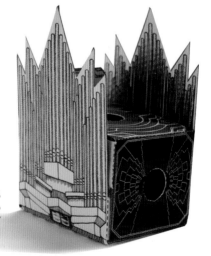

SEPTEMBER
26TH- WATERFALL AMPHITH
THANKSGIVING POINT, UT
28TH- STARLIGHT THE
KANSAS CITY, MO
30TH- ROY WILKIN
ST. PAUL, MN

2007 USA

Number of employees: 300+
Location: Cincinnati, OH
First year of business: 1919

LPK Cincinnati

When you hear the words "employee-owned branding agency," you likely think of a ten- to twenty-person shop at the most. Yet LPK has followed a model that has allowed it to emerge as the largest such agency in the world with offices all across the globe. Founded in 1919 (they still have the same phone number 89 years later) and then incorporated as LPK in 1983, they have built a framework of strategic thinking behind their creativity that re-invigorates brands in the tightly contested retail market. Their understanding of so many aspects of the industry under one roof gives them an edge few can match. Laid out into teams that allow the firm to compete on an even level with all of the corporate conglomerate agencies, it is clear that LPK takes pride in being the largest design firm in the world.

As Design Director Scott Burns explains, the challenge is rewarding when you can "create an expression that is unique, appropriate and emotively moving" for a product that will reach so many people. However, it can be tough to do in a business that moves so fast. "You only have hours sometimes to create a new design," he laughs, "as opposed to weeks, and you have to nail it … and you usually do!" On the Beauty side, Liz Grubow paints the opposite picture; "The work we do begins years ahead of a product launch. The length of time in development can be frustrating. You have a great idea; you want to get it out in the marketplace as quickly as possible." LPK makes the added time work to their benefit, though. "We really get to know the consumer that is targeted, sometimes very intimately. We go into consumer homes, see what products they use and how they use them. We go into their bedrooms, bathrooms and closets. You really get to know people that way. Once you have looked under their sink, you have bonded!" smiles Grubow.

"I love it when it's apparent that people really like the work," adds Creative Director Nathan Hendriks. "When women are stealing our designs from focus groups, I know we're onto something!"

Deeply involved in all aspects of a project, the LPK team will work hard to merge the "strengths of both structure and graphics," explains Burns. "We are constantly pushing our production partners to 'problem solve' with us to create techniques and finishes that will be unique and proprietary, that will set the package apart from competition, and that is consistent with the story and experience we are trying to create for the consumer," adds Grubow.

Mass-manufactured design can sometimes take it on the chin in industry reviews. "The design coming out of our office interacts with the lives of billions of people all over the world," explains Hendricks. He advocates for his packaging designers against the type of work so often filling the design annuals. "They work in a world where the bar is high, the competition is higher and the stakes are higher still. It's a skillet where they innovate or fry. The result is design that is much more relevant to its users and the surrounding culture. And, guess what? Sometimes it's beautiful."

Grubow sums up the appeal of working at LPK: "The work we do is global. To see a brand that we have worked on making an emotional connection with consumers around the world is extremely satisfying."

Q. What would be your dream packaging job? It can be an existing product or something not yet created for retail …
A. Burns: Beer!

Q. Do you still get excited when you see your design sitting on the shelf at a store?
A. Burns: If it's on shelf, then we're in the game! If the wrapper is in the garbage can, we made it!

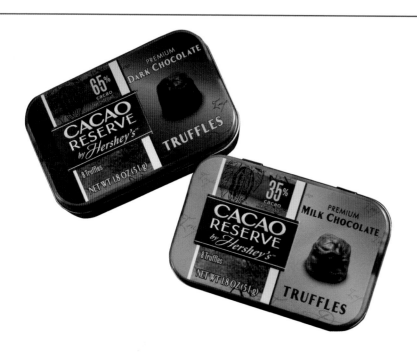

Studio: LPK

Art Directors: Ben Sauer, Jeff Hinkle

Designers: Victor Janzen, Scott Burns

Client: The Hershey Company

Client's Services: food producer

Illustrators: Ben Sauer, Scott Burns, Pete Haritos, Jeff Hinkle

Inks: six-color process

Printing Process: offset

Options Shown: numerous

In driving Hershey's portfolio expansion, the LPK team was empowered to "elevate the Hershey experience for premium chocolate," explains Burns. The end product was "definitely a collaborative effort," he smiles. After all, when was the last time you saw a seamless outlay of products with four illustrators credited?

Studio: LPK

Art Directors: Howard McIlvain, Andrew Tesnar

Designers: Andrew Tesnar, Jim Gabel

Client: Graeter's Ice Cream & Chocolate Co.

Client's Services: food producer

Illustrator: Andrew Tesnar

Inks: four-color process

Printing Process: flexography

Options Shown: numerous

"This design was a follow-up to the restaging of the Graeter's identity and a full reinvention of their ice cream packaging. It was actually pretty entertaining that one of the reasons that they wanted to redesign this was because Riverfront Stadium, where the Reds and Bengals played, had been imploded. Our client now felt that it was time and the bar was now dated," smiles Andrew Tesnar. The team kept "the nostalgic elements and tone for the brand," while taking advantage of modern techniques in design and printing.

Studio: LPK

Art Directors: Lia BraatenHager (P&G), Liz Grubow
(LPK Beauty), Tanya Blasko (P&G)

Designers: Heidi Gray, Chris Bautista, Susan Zinader,
Gina Tesnar, Frank Coyne

Package Designer: Heidi Hollman (Webb Scarlett deVlam)

Client: Proctor & Gamble

Client's Services: beauty products

Inks: six-color process, hot stamp

Printing Process: offset, hot stamp

Options Shown: numerous

In launching Olay White Radiance for the China Prestige Market, the P&G team, Webb Scarlett deVlam and the LPK Beauty team "logged enough frequent flyer miles to circumnavigate the globe multiple times," laughs Grubow from the LPK Beauty team. "The development of this work involved many trips to China to locate, evaluate and identify suppliers and printers. Additional long-term trips were needed to ensure that the design vision was executed with the utmost quality" the Olay brand demands. Sometimes the design is the easy part!

Studio: Payseur & Schmidt

Art Director: Jacob McMurray

Designer: Jacob McMurray

Client: Payseur & Schmidt

Client's Services: small-press publishing house

Illustrators: (box) Adam Grano (postcards) Andrio Abero, S. Britt, Guy Burwell, Art Chantry, Jacob Covey, Jon Daly, Carson Ellis, Dirk Fowler, Kaela Graham, Adam Grano, Chanda Helzer, Meg Hunt, Mike King, Karen Kirchhoff, Jeff Kleinsmith, Jesse LeDoux, The Little Friends of Printmaking, Corey Lunn, Jessica Lynch, Tara McPherson, Michael Michael Motorcycle, Heiko Müller, Julie Murphy, Martin Ontiveros, Lesley Reppeteaux, Jay Ryan, Diana Sudyka, Jason Van Hollander, Steven Weissman, Shawn Wolfe

Inks: (box) three spot inks on chipboard

(postcards) black ink

Printing Process: offset

Options Shown: one

"The Postcards of Doom postcard box set is a by-product of an extremely involved book project that I was art directing/designing for my super-nerd micropublishing house Payseur & Schmidt," explains Jacob McMurray. "*The Darkening Garden* by John Clute is a series of thirty interconnected short essays about the fundamental motifs in the horror literary genre since 1750. I decided to treat the book more as an exhibition, and so I decided to pair each of the motifs that Clute discusses with a different artist or illustrator or designer. I had asked Adam Grano, resident designer at Fantagraphics, to illustrate a 'sash' to surround *The Darkening Garden* book, so I thought it'd be good to retain that continuity and have Adam illustrate the box. Since Payseur & Schmidt is a strange combination of ghetto and fabulous, I chose a chipboard for the box. All that, and a snappy title, and we have liftoff."

Studio: The Small Stakes

Art Director: Jason Munn

Designer: Jason Munn

Client: Asthmatic Kitty Records

Printing Process: two spot colors

Options Shown: one

"The design is an interpretation of the album's title—*First Light's Freeze*," explains Jason Munn. The second full-length album from the Castanets is adorned with a "white burst acting as the 'freeze' spreading over the leaves," according to Munn. Munn is now designing the band's third full-length album.

Studio: Cold Open

Art Directors: John Peed, Gardner DeFranceaux

Designer: Gardner DeFranceaux

Client: Sony Pictures Home Entertainment, Abe Lugioyo

Client's Services: Meme Fehmers

Illustrator: Gardner DeFranceaux, Jon Davis

Inks: four-color process

Printing Process: offset

Options Shown: sixteen

Working on the project, John Peed noted that "not a lot of photography existed, as the films were older in the collection. We submitted a few illustrations done in-house, and it got everyone at Sony really excited. Most of the illustrations were done by hand and then scanned in and colorized on the computer. We then added layers and layers of textures. The final product is a unique mixture of designs coming together to showcase the iconic Buster Keaton."

Studio: Post Typography

Art Directors: Bruce Willen, Nolen Strals

Designers: Bruce Willen, Nolen Strals

Client: Double Dagger

Client's Services: record label

Inks: four-color process

Printing Process: offset, silkscreen

Options Shown: one

Sometimes taking known images and turning their use into something altogether different can create a jarring effect mixed with odd familiarity. "The second album by the post-punk band Double Dagger—*Ragged Rubble*—features louder, noisier, and more politically charged songs than on the band's previous releases," says Bruce Willen. "Reflecting these changes (and the drummer's love of maps), we created a shattered composition by rearranging America's fifty states." The "abrasive color scheme" was created using the studio's beloved local teams in Baltimore: Ravens purple and Orioles orange. The theme "is continued onto the back cover, where the band name is drawn as if each letter were a state."

Modern Dog <small>Seattle</small>

Number of employees: 4.5
Location: Seattle, WA
First year of business: 1987

"In 1995, we got a phone call from someone who claimed to be Billy Gibbons from ZZ Top. He said he loved our Modern Dog Poster Playing Cards, first edition, and was in the recording studio playing with them. Mike thought it was a friend playing a joke, so we told him if he was really Billy Gibbons to take a photo and send it to us. The very next day, FedEx arrived with a whole bunch of Billy Gibbons/ZZ Top swag. We've kept the framed photo of Billy holding our cards in our bathroom ever since. True story," laughs Robynne Raye. From the early days she spent with partner Mike Strassburger designing Japanese skis and snowboards, Raye had no idea how big a role packaging design would play in their future. She speculates that between assignments and commissions on existing products, "60 percent of our revenue comes from packaging."

Having the freedom to write the copy for many of the projects is a major draw for the Modern Dog crew. "We have a lot of fun writing copy and naming products for Blue Q and Olive, a 'green' dog products company. Both companies embrace humor and fun in their master marketing plan," says Raye. "Jay Leno has also mentioned our Blue Q products on his show—Handz Off Anti Masturbatory Cream and Mother Teresa Breath Spray are two that we know of. He even read all the copy of the latter, and Mike was in heaven for like a whole week."

When working for their first corporate client, K2, Raye says, "Even though we were naming products and writing a lot of copy, I don't think we ever thought we were focusing or doing anything specialized. For us, it was just graphic design." Their early success in those arenas did not go unnoticed, as clients in need of innovative and hip packaging started beating down the door. Their quirky brand of humor has shown up on endearing pieces worldwide and contains a voice that is solely theirs.

Their worldwide appeal is apparent. "We have a designer friend, Åsa Sandlund, who works at Nordstrom and is originally from Sweden. When she went home to visit, she told us she found these funny 'Swedish products' and brought them back to us because she thought we would like them. Turns out the items she thought were Swedish souvenirs were products we designed for Blue Q," laughs Raye.

This quirkiness doesn't make its way into the production cycle, though. Sticking to what works and deferring to the client rule the day. "Mitch

[Nash] at Blue Q is really good about ironing out all the mechanical details of a product. Often, we have input regarding the scent of a soap, or the shape of a car air freshener. We don't do too many tricky printing techniques or fancy die cuts, so the challenge of printing and finishing doesn't typically apply to us," admits Raye. "We stick with simple because it's what we know. With certain kinds of clients like Shout! Factory, we don't have a voice or control in regards to the printer or fabricator they choose. All those details are worked out on their end. One thing we have learned the hard way is that when designing CDs or DVDs, always plan for at least a 20 percent dot gain because the printer will always go darker versus lighter. When was the last time you saw a CD package—or anything for that matter—printed too light?"

Unintentionally selling cool as a commodity, the Modern Dog pack continues to work the same way they have for years. Talented designers surrounded by five doggies, electric guitars and an old-school waxer for paste-up along with plenty of things to draw with to clutter the office and keep those funky packages coming to you.

Q. What would be your dream packaging job? It can be an existing product or something not yet created for retail …
A. Personally, I think it would be great fun to design wine labels. It would be a bonus if the winery was located in the south of France or Tuscany, and they wanted to fly me out to sample the wine on location. I can't think of a better way to do research. After that, pretty much anything we work on with Blue Q or Olive—both produce great, fun products. And the people behind the company are super cool.

Q. Do you still get excited when you see your design sitting on the shelf at a store?
A. Sure. It's still exciting and fun. We especially like to see our products in use, like when we spot a "wtf? Bush" bumper sticker on a car driving down the road. It makes us giggle.

Studio: Modern Dog

Art Director: Robert Zwiebel

Designer: Robert Zwiebel

Client: Blue Q

Client's Services: retail products

Inks: four-color process

Printing Process: offset

Options Shown: four

While brainstorming for another Blue Q project, "Rob showed an idea that was just a rainbow. He was trying to explain the rainbow idea to everyone, and during a pause he just blurted out, 'I'm not gay, I just like rainbows!'" laughs Robynne Raye. His Hawaiian upbringing during the 1970s and early 1980s was to blame, as "everybody had rainbow stickers on the back of their car windows. So Rob has always liked rainbows (and seagulls, butterflies, puffy clouds, guys on skates, etc.). And he's not gay," adds Raye.

Studio: Modern Dog

Art Directors: Michael Strassburger, Mitch Nash

Designers: Michael Strassburger, Vittorio Costarella

Client: Blue Q

Client's Services: retail products

Photographer: Meg Paradise

Illustrators: Michael Strassburger, Vittorio Costarella, Junichi Tsuneoka

Inks: four-color process

Printing Process: offset

Options Shown: a dozen or so, for all five car air fresheners

Working with Blue Q, the Modern Dog crew often proposes fully thought-out new products or extensions of existing lines. This includes the copy and naming as well as the look. In this case, "all product names and most of the copy are by Michael Strassburger, except for Little Fatman, which is by Vittorio Costarella," says Robynne Raye. "The Cat Butt freshener has been a big seller since 2004, to the extent that we have sold between 1.5 and 2 million dollars of Cat Butt stuff." It has some new competition, though, as Road Rage is moving like middle-finger-waving hotcakes.

Studio: Modern Dog

Art Directors: Robynne Raye, Michael Strassburger

Designer: Meg Paradise

Client: Shout! Factory

Client's Services: music and entertainent

Photographer: Meg Paradise and others

Illustrator: Meg Paradise

Inks: four-color process

Printing Process: offset

Options Shown: three

"Cowboy Jack is a really unique and eccentric writer-producer-musician who was close friends with the late Johnny Cash," explains Raye. "Jack wrote several hits, including *Ballad of a Teenage Queen* in 1957, and that was soon followed by a number one hit for Johnny, *Guess Things Happen That Way* in 1958. This DVD is really engaging, and anyone interested in Nashville music history knows Jack Clement as a legend." The firm gave the eccentric performer a suitable quirky package to house his story.

Studio: Modern Dog

Art Director: Robynne Raye

Designer: Robynne Raye

Client: Olive

Client's Services: green dog products

Logo: Vittorio Costarella

Inks: four-color process

Printing Process: offset

Options Shown: one

After creating the product name and doing all of the copywriting, it only seemed fitting that Raye perform the product testing as well for this canine bathing product. "The stuff smells so good I actually took a bath with it, so now we can say it was tested on humans first," she laughs. The packaging intentionally uses minimal amounts of recycled paper and glue and is printed using soy ink.

Studio: Modern Dog

Art Director: Michael Strassburger

Designers: Michael Strassburger, Meg Paradise

Client: Shout! Factory

Client's Services: music and entertainment

Inks: four-color process

Printing Process: offset

Options Shown: three

When given a performer's name that might be a tad awkward, Modern Dog makes the most of it. I can honestly say that I didn't think it possible that I would feature a piece where the title had three hyphens in it, but in working the name into the negative space of the jacket, the design perfectly reflects the comedic stylings contained within.

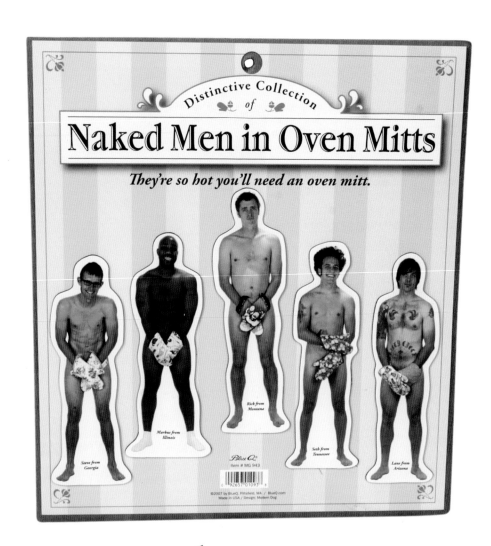

Studio: Modern Dog

Art Director: Michael Strassburger

Designer: Michael Strassburger

Client: Blue Q

Client's Services: retail products

Photographer: Ron Carraher

Inks: four-color process

Printing Process: offset

Options Shown: one

Sometimes the challenge isn't coming up with a concept, it's executing it. "Mike came up with this idea and then realized he had to find the models," giggles Robynne Raye. "So at 1 A.M. he put an ad on Craigslist, and by 9 A.M. the next morning he had over a hundred guys willing to take it all off for a hundred dollars. He was shocked. A lot of the potential models sent naked pictures of themselves (eewww), and we recognized one of the guys in the photos as one of our design students (hee hee). Luckily, he had no shame when he realized it was us. Our good friend Ron Carraher (a.k.a. Figus Upshaw) took the photos. My favorite guy is the one who didn't take his socks off."

Studio: Ron Liberti

Art Director: Ron Liberti

Designer: Ron Liberti

Client: The Ghost of Rock

Client's Services: punk rock band

Photographer/Illustrator: Ron Liberti

Inks: four-color process

Printing Process: offset

Options Shown: one

Compiling a release of his '90s punk rock band The Ghost of Rock, Ron Liberti looked around the room for inspiration … or was it perspiration? "I decided to take a photo of my old Converse sneakers and hand draw the stink coming off them in the band name, as I felt it really captured what our sound 'looked' like," he says. The idea of heat and smell lifting off of an object was continued on the interior with an old photo of football fans trying to keep warm in the stands.

Studio: Methane Studios
Art Director: Jay Rogers
Designer: Robert Lee
Illustrator: Robert Lee
Client: Cartoon Network
Client's Services: cable TV network
Inks: four-color process
Printing Process: offset
Options Shown: one

Working to provide "maximum-strength stress relief" along with maximum humor, the Methane gang helped Cartoon Network package up their batch of stress balls made in the mold of the channel's top animated stars.

Studio: Methane Studios

Art Director: Robert Lee

Designer: Robert Lee

Illustrator: Robert Lee

Client: Caddle

Client's Services: rock band

Inks: four-color process

Printing Process: offset

Options Shown: one

"Caddle is a good ol' southern rock band," explains Robert Lee. "What could I do but design a package to reflect the genre with skulls, a bottle of Jäger and crisscrossed racing flags?" Southern rock band imagery? Check! Methane manages to give consumers an instant picture of the Alabama country meets punk meets hard-luck tales that they will find inside.

Ham my ass!

Chewy CHEWING GUM™

Classic Fruit Flavor

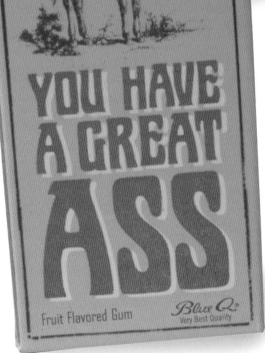

8 ass-kicking pieces
artificial flavor

YOU HAVE A GREAT ASS

Fruit Flavored Gum

Blue Q®
Very Best Quality

It's Not PMS

It's You

"We had a blast on these puppies!" declares Lee. Given a chance to do the fun illustrative design they love—and some copywriting to boot—they lapped up every minute of the chance to produce gum packaging for Blue Q. There was even an odd candy connection to one of the models: "The dog for the PMS gum was named Cane," laughs Lee.

Studio: Methane Studios

Art Director: Mitch Nash

Designers: Robert Lee, Mark McDevitt

Photographer: Mike Koller

Illustrators: Mark McDevitt, Robert Lee

Client: Blue Q

Client's Services: retail products

Inks: four-color process

Printing Process: offset

Options Shown: numerous

Studio: Methane Studios

Art Director: Robert Lee

Designer: Robert Lee

Illustrator: Robert Lee

Client: RCA

Client's Services: record label

Inks: four-color process

Printing Process: offset

Options Shown: numerous

As self-described "enormous fans of the band Traffic," Methane was truly honored to hear that Steve Winwood himself had seen their work in a book and personally requested that they get the honors of packaging *The Last Great Traffic Jam*.

Studio: Methane Studios

Art Director: Mitch Nash

Designer: Robert Lee

Illustrator: Robert Lee

Client: Blue Q

Client's Services: retail products

Inks: four-color process

Printing Process: offset

Options Shown: numerous

For this project, how could the firm pass up the chance to "draw two pigs," as they put it? Plus, Lee admits to a certain pleasure in "putting the word 'asshole' next to Dick Cheney's face." Making air fresheners for Blue Q gives the firm the type of assignment they value the most, when they can design and illustrate in conjunction with one another. They love the air fresheners so much they recommended the company "make one that smells like Methane!"

Studio: Compass Design

Art Director: Mitchell Lindgren

Designers: Mitchell Lindgren, Tom Arthur

Client: Daddy Sam's

Client's Services: food producer

Inks: four-color process

Printing Process: offset

Options Shown: three

Working with "a small client with no food manufacturing experience at all, Compass developed the
solutions based on the name Daddy Sam's, which
came from the client's grandfather," explains Mitch
Lindgren. "The owner grew up in Texas and expe-
rienced the family barbecue recipe so many times
and just loved it." The firm was taken by the story
that "at every meal, his grandfather insisted they
'Just slop it on!' [It only seemed appropriate that the]
photo on the label is his grandfather—Daddy Sam."
The work for the client didn't end at the design stage,
though. "After we designed the label, we got him
a printer, a food manufacturer and a glass bottle
supplier. It was hands-on from the beginning until
it hit the shelves," explains Lindgren.

Studio: Compass Design

Art Director: Mitchell Lindgren

Designers: Mitchell Lindgren, Tom Arthur

Client: August Schell's Brewing Company

Client's Services: brewing company

Inks: five-color process

Printing Process: flexography

Options Shown: three

"Snowstorm Beer is created with a different recipe each year by the brewmaster at August Schell's," explains Lindgren. "No one knows what the recipe will be, except for the brewmaster. This one-of-a-kind seasonal beer offered each winter has many fans who can't wait each year to sample a new brew." Knowing that anticipation runs high, the team at Compass like to hold true to their overall packaging look for the company, but also give it that special touch. Working from the family architecture they created for August Schell's other beers, and of course, the time of year it is produced, they definitely deliver.

Studio: Hollis BC Design

Art Director: Don Hollis

Designer: Angela Villareal

Client: Love Culture

Client's Services: women's clothing company

Inks: Pantone 877 Silver

Printing Process: silkscreen

Options Shown: one

Special Production Techniques: (case) logotype
etching on steel plate, computer-cut routed
3 Form Lexan material with hex bolts and rubber
spacers. (jacket) custom tailored red neoprene
(surf wetsuit) material.

The team at Hollis had previously developed naming, positioning and brand strategies for Love Culture clothing, and now they needed "an enticing program to garner media interest and secure premium store locations at high-end destination retail centers," says Don Hollis. "The brand development and interior architecture are groundbreaking for this market segment. The architecture is very open and transparent, revealing layers of discovery within the retail space. We felt this was an important differentiator for the space and should be reflected in the packaging. A bold red case serves as a wrapper to build anticipation regarding the contents, and the transparent case continues to tease viewers as the presentation is unveiled."

Funny (now) story: "The case had to be completely taken apart and reassembled with extra spacers to hold a last-minute client addition of extra presentation panels," Hollis laughs.

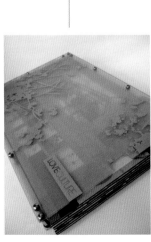

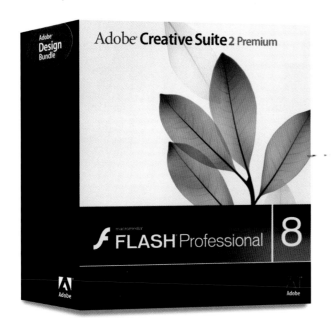

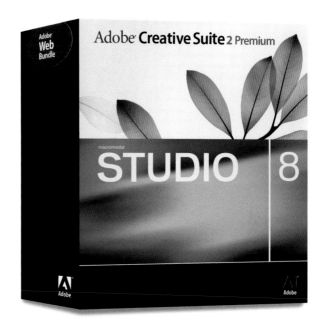

Studio: AdamsMorioka

Art Directors: Sean Adams, Noreen Morioka, Volker Dürre

Designers: Volker Dürre, Monica Schlaug

Client: Adobe Systems Incorporated

Client's Services: software company

Inks: four-color process, spot PMS

Printing Process: offset

Options Shown: three, refined to one final

Special Production Techniques: overall satin aqueous varnish

Blending two companies is difficult to accomplish in a single box, admits the team at AdamsMorioka. "This was an interim packaging solution created after the merging of Adobe and Macromedia, but before the release of CS3. The challenge was to work within the existing Adobe shape, structure and format, but to represent both companies' software. We created a band system that clearly promotes both the Adobe and Macromedia components," explains Noreen Morioka.

Studio: Imagehaus

Art Director: Imagehaus

Client: Imagehaus

Client's Services: design firm

Inks: four-color process, four PMS, two PMS

Printing Process: offset, screen printing

Options Shown: one

"Serving as something fun to mail to clients (both potential and current) as well as a gift for friends and family, the challenge was to create a promotion that wouldn't end up in the trash," explain Jay Miller and Stephanie Wetzell. "The functioning clock is value-added and has a different face for each month of the year to engage the recipient and remind them of us year-round. It was mailed in a screen-printed shipping box (created by silkscreen, one at a time, with love). Many clients e-mailed or phoned to say how much they enjoyed the promotion and additional requests poured in as word of the clock spread."

Studio: Imagehaus

Art Director: Imagehaus

Client: Wilsons Leather

Client's Services: leather retailer

Inks: four-color process

Printing Process: offset

Options Shown: five

"The client really wanted to elevate the quality of the Wilsons Leather brand wallets against the other brand-named wallets currently available," explain Jay Miller and Stephanie Wetzell. "Before, the Wilsons Leather wallets were in a cardboard box or no box at all." Setting out to house the quality goods in an embossed tin, the end result "increased sales for the retailer and drew more attention to the Wilsons Leather brand."

Studio: Imagehaus
Art Director: Imagehaus
Client: Schmidty's
Client's Services: barbershop
Inks: two PMS
Printing Process: offset
Options Shown: three

"Schmidty's provided a hip barbershop experience—damn nice haircuts, manly rubdowns and no-frills pricing," say Jay Miller and Stephanie Wetzell. "We created a family of logos inspired by beer, sports and cigars, then translated these into a series of beer coasters with services and pricing on the reverse. The result is a brochure chock-full of testosterone." Keeping that manly feel going, "Our gift card system positions Schmidty's as the ideal gift for existing and potential Schmidtheads. Packaging these with boxers proclaiming 'It's a man's thing' makes a nice gift set."

Studio: Imagehaus

Art Director: Imagehaus

Client: Kuhlman Company

Client's Services: clothing company

Inks: four-color process, two PMS

Printing Process: offset, flexography

Options Shown: numerous

"An Anglo-Italian clothing line for those wanting to 'stand apart' from the crowd, Kuhlman Company needed a giveaway/guerrilla marketing piece that would launch their latest fall line of fabrics used in the making of men's and women's shirts," explain Jay Miller and Stephanie Wetzell. Creating a memory game proved useful not only in "making your wardrobe selection when you got home, but it also gives your kids, or even the kid in you, something to do when taking a break. We wanted to get across the idea that there is something for everyone, and that you may just want to collect them all." These were given away in-store with a purchase, and person to person on the streets in new markets.

memory game

At Kuhlman we want you to be real smart. Spread these discs out with the patterns face down. Now, take turns with a partner flipping over two at a time. If they match place them in your area. The person with the most matches after all have been paired up, wins.

kuhlmancompany.com

Studio: Imagehaus

Art Director: Imagehaus

Client: Pagoda

Client's Services: salon and spa

Inks: four-color process

Printing Process: offset

Options Shown: three

"Tom Schmidt, an icon in the salon and spa industry, was launching a new five-star spa experience offering unprecedented services and amenities," explain Jay Miller and Stephanie Wetzell. "We created the positioning platform, Zen-inspired brand name, clean contemporary logo and business system." They then ensured that experience was realized in all aspects. "Personalized guest inter-actions are an integral part of the premium experience at Pagoda. Our family of gift boxes and shopping bags introduced a pattern reminiscent of this premium cache and to represent the artful, delicate nuances of the brand."

Studio: Wade Graphic Design

Art Director: Rick Wade

Client: Clean Ones Corporation

Client's Services: cleaning products

Inks: four spot colors

Printing Process: flexography

Options Shown: five

"This was designed during a printing transition for the client," explains Wade. "Poly bag printing for past projects was limited to the center 80 percent area of the bag for printing. This was one of the first projects that we were able to print the entire area of the bag, edge to edge, with ink." Wade adds that the firm had "a lot of input on the product name. The client initially wanted to name this product line 'Pizzazz.' This sounded nice, but in a printed form, it has several problems, not the least of which that it looks a lot like 'Pizza' and with all the 'z's, the brand name is very sharp."

Index of Contributors